COACHING
COMPETENCIES
and
CORPORATE
LEADERSHIP

COACHING
COMPETENCIES
and
CORPORATE
LEADERSHIP

TRACEY WEISS WITH SHARYN KOLBERG

S_L^t

ST. LUCIE PRESS

A CRC Press Company
Boca Raton   London   New York   Washington, D.C.

Library of Congress Cataloging-in-Publication Data

Weiss, Tracey Bernstein.
    Coaching competencies and corporate leadership / Tracey B. Weiss ;
with Sharyn Kolberg.
       p. cm.
Includes bibliographical references and index.
    ISBN 1-57444-319-4 (alk. paper)
    1. Leadership. 2. Mentoring in business. I. Kolberg, Sharyn. II.
Title.
    HD57.7.W4537 2003
    658.4′092—dc21   2002037056

Visit the CRC Press Web site at www.crcpress.com

© 2003 by CRC Press LLC
St. Lucie Press is an imprint of CRC Press LLC

No claim to original U.S. Government works
International Standard Book Number 1-57444-319-4
Library of Congress Card Number 2002037056
Printed in the United States of America 1 2 3 4 5 6 7 8 9 0
Printed on acid-free paper

Dedication

In memory of Kenneth G. Martin

1950–2000

My friend and coach

Contents

Preface

At heart, I have always been both a teacher and a student. I have been fortunate to continue to meet a variety of people and have traveled to many interesting places in both capacities over many years. One thing I have found to be true: learning has kept me stimulated, curious, and optimistic about life and its possibilities.

Learning takes many forms, but the most powerful is the learning we gain from direct exposure to other people. Whether we know it or not, many of those people to whom we have been exposed have been coaches. Sometimes they are parents or teachers or community leaders. Sometimes they are friends or colleagues. All of us, if we have been lucky, have grown from our experience with these early coaches in our lives. Coaching is about connections, relationships that endure and make a difference to who we are and who we might become. A good coach can open a door that we otherwise might not see, might not walk through.

Coaching is especially important in the workplace, where people are measured on their perceived performance. Successful performance, especially for leaders, is more a matter of how these leaders impact others than one of technical expertise. By the time someone is in a leadership role, he or she is the conductor rather than the musician in the symphony of business results.

The subject of this book is how you can help leaders be more effective. While I talk about applying the same rigor to coaching that you would to other business processes, coaching is ultimately about the personal connection. It is not just a set of "tools" and "skills;" it is, in the end, letting other people know that you care about them and their success.

Coaching is the art of giving back. You are investing in someone else and seeing the world through his or her eyes. It is a reciprocal relationship that enriches the life experiences of both people in the coaching relationship. I hope you feel inspired by this book, and will pick up some new ideas to make coaching as exciting and rewarding as I know it can be.

The Author

Dr. Tracey B. Weiss is the founder of Tracey Weiss Associates — Consulting in Executive and Organizational Performance. She specializes in executive coaching and organization development. Her work focuses on selection and development processes, utilizing multi-rater feedback, team-building, and performance management programs that produce bottom line results. Recent clients reflect a broad spectrum in both the public and private sector, including  Campbell Soup, ARAMARK, University of California Healthcare System, The Federal Reserve Board, Merck, QVC, City of Philadelphia, Adventis Pasteur Pharmaceuticals, Vanguard, Sesame Street, and the University of Pennsylvania. Dr. Weiss received the Quality Consultant Award from Union Carbide in recognition for her work in developing their performance management program.

Prior to starting her firm, Dr. Weiss was a vice president with the Hay Group, where she held numerous leadership positions in human resources planning and development for over 10 years. She also previously held human resource management positions at both GlaxoSmithKline and ARAMARK.

Dr. Weiss was previously an assistant professor of communication at the University of New Hampshire, where she received a fellowship from the National Endowment of the Humanities. She earned her Ph.D. in organizational communication from Temple University. Dr. Weiss is a member of both the Philadelphia Human Resources Planning Group and the Organization Development Network. She is also on the board of directors of the Philadelphia Theatre Company.

Her book, *Reengineering Performance Management: Breakthroughs in Achieving Strategies through People,* co-authored with Franklin Hartle, was published in 1997 by St. Lucie Press. In addition, Dr. Weiss has been featured in publications such as *The Human Resource Executive* and has been published in *HR Focus.* She authored a chapter on "Performance Management" in the *Compensation Handbook,* 3rd edition, McGraw-Hill, January 2000. She also authored a chapter on "Solving the Performance Management Dilemma: One Size Does Not Fit All" in *The Executive Handbook on Compensation* in 2001.

Acknowledgments

Writing this book reaffirmed the importance of relationships in a very personal way for me. Two valued professionals whom I am lucky to have as friends and colleagues helped me get this book off the ground and were instrumental in the initial stages of this project. Jean Kirshenbaum, a communications and public relations consultant, worked with me through the process of writing the proposal that led to this book. She also helped me in a hands-on way in conducting and analyzing all the executive interviews that we used as research throughout the book. Judith Schuster, a leading organization development consultant, was a guiding light and provided thought leadership to the first section of the book, which establishes the coaching process. Judith was instrumental in defining the particular issues that are involved in coaching people of different generations and are elaborated on in Chapter 9. Judith worked selflessly to help me get this project off the ground, and I hope the finished work reflects her contribution.

I had the privilege of interviewing a number of senior executives and leading consultants whose wisdom and experience illuminate many of the points I make throughout these chapters. In particular, my heartfelt thanks go to Tom Downs, John Hunter, Bill McGrath, and Beth Rubino at QVC; John Nackley and Tom Dimmick at InterMetro Industries, a division of Emerson; Mel Ming and Jerry Harvey at Sesame Workshop; Jim Kenney at Campbell Soup; Ray Welsch at Aramark; Catharine Newberry at Aventis Pasteur; and Dorothy Sumonovitch of the Gestalt Institute for their time and contributions.

Special thanks are given to two other contributors whom I have had the privilege of learning from as colleagues and being inspired by as friends. Both Renee Booth and Ellen Petersen supported me in this project from beginning to end, were sources of encouragement, and kept reminding me that this book was a worthwhile endeavor when the road to completion seemed long.

Sharyn Kolberg has been a terrific collaborator and has helped me find my voice for this project. She is not only an excellent and patient editor, but she has coached me through this process by asking gentle but probing questions that provided the book's focus and structure. This book would not be what it is without her partnership.

Thanks to my family — Bill Goldberg, Zach Goldberg, Aaron Weiss, Shirley Bernstein, and Ethel Goldberg — for always being in my corner and for being my first line of defense against distractions that would have sidetracked me from completing this project.

Finally, I want to acknowledge all the coaches who have been pivotal at various points in my life. I hope this book does them justice and that I can pass on to others what they passed on to me. The book is dedicated to one of them.

THE CASE FOR COACHING COMPETENCIES

Chapter 1

Leadership Development

"I absolutely believe that people, unless coached, never reach their maximum capability."

Bob Nardelli, *CEO Home Depot*

Great coaches make great leaders. Yet great leaders are not always great coaches. Jim Kenney was one of those great coach leaders and the kind of person everyone wanted to work for. When he went to work as the president of the Sales Division of Campbell Soup, the company had just survived an agonizing decade of wringing profits from cost-cutting. The team he inherited felt uncertain and apprehensive. Jim came on board and took his time getting to know his executive team and getting out to meet key customers. He let it be known that he was there to listen and learn. During his first year, he spent significant time really getting to know his executive team and asking them to collaborate with him in establishing a three-year plan. They also worked together to build a set of core values that clarified what the Sales Division and the company stood for. These values became the foundation for guiding the decisions with customers, employees, and shareholders. Jim then identified the core competencies that would serve as success criteria; these competencies were directly linked to the company's core values and the new long-range business plan. Jim took his time building relationships with each of his direct reports, talking to each of them about what the competencies meant in terms of success and strengths. He encouraged them to let go of the limiting beliefs that isolated them from each other and limited their contributions to their own functional areas. Jim emphasized the fact that each one of his team was a wealth of information and that he expected each person to share best practices with one another.

This was not easy as it sounded. Several of the remaining executive team members had interviewed for the job that Jim was eventually hired for and were unsure about Jim's style. His people-development philosophy was a far cry from the hard-nosed, top-down management style that had characterized the Sales Division for years, and the team was doubtful that Jim's style would work in the increasingly competitive marketplace they were facing. Jim knew that it would take some time for his people to see that he had the integrity to act on the beliefs and values they all had agreed were important. As time went on, people began to see that Jim was the real deal. The remaining executives who clung to the old culture, making decisions secretly to favor a few trusted and fanning the flames of blame and mistrust, realized that their time was over and left the organization. The executive team began to open up and connect to each other and their customers in new ways. Innovation and a new spirit of hope sprang up like a hidden wellspring in the team.

What did Jim do to win his team's support and inspire trust and respect? Jim was a great leader because he was a great coach. He took the time to listen and understand the war stories that were the collective history of his beleaguered team without judging or criticizing the way things were in the past, and he didn't stop there. He infused his team with a sense of hope and possibility because he demonstrated credibility from his own years of experience, articulated a philosophy and vision for the future, and most importantly, grounded the organization in the competencies required to ensure business results. Developing talent was a priority for Jim. He believed that if you invest in your people they will respond to that and give the discretionary effort needed to make a quantum difference.

The power of Jim's coaching — coaching for competencies — comes from the fact that it focuses and aligns individual performance while unifying an organizational culture around the behaviors required for success.

In this book, I am going to share with you how to coach the leaders who work for you and how to build leadership equity in your organization. The title of the book, *Coaching Competencies and Corporate Leadership,* describes the basic value proposition of the book. It reflects my belief that coaching for competencies is the approach that works best for leaders coaching other leaders, because competencies link behavioral change directly to business results. When you are coaching for competencies, you dramatically impact the opportunity to align leadership behavior. As a result, all oars are pulling in the same direction. The language of competencies is a powerful communication tool.

When used at senior levels in the coaching process, competencies provide a common framework and vocabulary for describing people and jobs. Competencies put everyone on the same page regarding what it takes to be successful. Coaching for competencies can ensure that leaders have a uniform way to communicate expectations and results achieved. Starting at the top ensures that competencies get woven into the culture and used as a common perspective when hiring people, developing them, appraising their work efforts, rewarding them, and promoting them to the next role. Leaders who have been coached for competencies are more likely to become coaches themselves with the people who report to them; this can become a powerful vehicle for changing a company culture.

I suggest that you should capitalize on the investment you have already made in your people. I discuss the high cost of replacing leaders who leave the organization and how coaching for competencies can make a dramatic difference in both the retention and performance of senior executives. Some of you may have already introduced competency models into your organization, but you may not have effectively integrated them into your coaching practices. Reading this book can help you reap the rewards of the consultant and staff time already spent on developing these competency models and ensure that your leaders understand why these competencies are critical to your business success.

Who Should Read This Book?

This book is written primarily for senior executives who want to coach other leaders who work with and for them. It is also for managers who are concerned about developing the next generation of leaders for their organization, or to put it another way, developing the bench strength for their organizations. Consultants who are involved in coaching and want to link their work more directly to a competency approach can also find relevant ideas here. Increasingly, competency-based models are a popular approach for selecting and developing human capital in organizations of all sizes. Those of you who have already developed competency models for your organization can find specific suggestions on how to develop leaders around these competencies. Those who have not yet considered a competency focus can discover the rationale and payoff for you and your business in taking this approach.

In the pages that follow, you learn how to "push the pause button" at times and have coaching conversations that can make your successful leaders even more successful, and you see how to redirect the efforts of leaders who are struggling. This is not a time-consuming process, but it does call for the same rigor and discipline that you use in other parts of the business. Coaching for competencies delivers bottom-line results and a workplace where people can reach their full potential.

Research supports the effectiveness of coaching for leadership development. People who feel valued tend to increase their commitment and productivity, which results in employee and customer retention. In fact, research done by Manchester Consulting shows that coaching dramatically improves working relationships between supervisors, direct reports, and their respective teams, demonstrating a 5:1 return on investment.

The Changing Role of Coaching

Coaching has been around in some form for hundreds of years. Since the Middle Ages, apprentices have bartered their time and labor to obtain the skills and knowledge of a craft or business. Many businesses today accept interns (often unpaid) who do the grunt work in order to learn from their elders. When businesses got serious about coaching higher-level employees, however, the job was usually outsourced to consultants for the most senior-level managers. The work, primarily provided by psychologists, was a combination of intellectual and psychological assessment and confidential therapeutic interactions. Such assessment and coaching was typically used for succession planning and/or to help a "difficult" person fit in with other senior-level executives. Problem employees were viewed as having personality issues; problems were rarely described in behavioral terms.

Times have changed. The business climate has become more competitive and the workforce less loyal. Retention is a competitive strategy, and employees at all levels expect to be treated with respect and included in decisions that affect them. How leaders treat their employees, peers, and customers has a direct correlation to bottom-line results.

While external executive coaches are increasingly used among senior management ranks, the coaching role is too important to relegate to outside resources alone. As a manager, you need to understand your role as a coach and know how to inspire others and direct their performance to higher levels. You don't need to go it alone, though. Outside executive coaches, as well as internal staff in your human resources department, can be effective partners with you in the coaching process.

When senior executives coach, the coaching typically focuses on tactical issues to resolve an immediate business problem. While this type of day-to-day problem-solving is important, it doesn't necessarily address the deeper issues of executive development that include how leaders see themselves or are seen by others. As a result, the leader being coached doesn't always "see the forest for the trees." The senior executive may fix the immediate problem but may not see the overall pattern and the impact on his own longer-term career success.

In fact, leaders often lament that coaching is something they know is important yet they don't take the time or find it difficult to get relationships with their people jump-started. People who should be asking for feedback are reluctant to do so because they think that it will make them seem weak. People who should be giving feedback don't always take the time or don't feel that they have established the right kind of relationship with the person who needs coaching. This leads to avoidance of the coaching relationship at senior levels.

The bottom-line implications of the issue are clear when we recognize that the most frequent reason people leave companies is a lack of confidence in their leaders or a poor relationship with their immediate supervisors. The cost of turnover is high, and in the executive ranks it can reach 150% of a leader's annual salary.

What can you do about this? The old answer, of course, is to send your leaders to training courses in management development. Companies have traditionally offered training programs as the key resource to educate managers in leadership responsibilities. The staggering sum of over $60 billion is spent in North America alone on training. Yet when it comes to training in management skills, there is little evidence that the skills and abilities that are taught are sustained over time. Part of the reason for this is that, unlike coaching, when you send someone to a training program you are delegating leadership development to others. Without follow-up coaching on the job, any learning that took place in the seminar tends to dissipate over time. The article "Effects on Productivity in a Public Agency," published in *Public Personnel Management* (1997), cited that in case studies where coaching was added to training, productivity rose 88%. Without coaching, productivity rose only 22%.

Coaching offers leaders more active support. The message from the organization is, "We believe in you, we are investing in you, and we are providing coaching to encourage your success." When we interviewed Tom Kaney, vice president of human resources at Glaxo/SmithKline, he told us that he views coaching as vital to the development of their executive team. He recommends a structured process of coaching for all new executives at the vice president level or higher, whether promoted from within or hired from outside of the company. For example, in the Sales Division coaching is now required, and new executives are not only coached by their own line managers but are provided with an external professional executive coach for one year.

If you make the investment in coaching, you are forming a powerful partnership between you and the leader you coach. Coaching is fundamentally a relationship, and a good coach has a personal investment in the process and in the success of the leader being coached. A coach can help people make choices, determine priorities, consider decisions, assess risks and opportunities, change behavior, and generally think through the personal dilemmas of work.

Assumptions That Hold Us Back from Being Better Coaches

If coaching leaders is critically important, why does it not always get the attention it deserves? Part of the reason is the belief, sometimes unconsciously held, that leaders are born and not made. Leadership is falsely viewed as an innate set of characteristics that one either does or does not have. Some organizations take a "sink or swim" approach and place leaders in challenging situations, sometimes even when management knows that these leaders will face obstacles for which they are unprepared, and see if they can meet the challenge on their own. This approach to leadership development feels right to senior executives who climbed the corporate ladder by going through their own trials by fire and therefore assume that their successors should face similar tests.

Waiting to see who will sink and who will swim does not yield optimal results. The cost is high, both to the individuals and the organizations that hire them. Recruiting leaders into executive positions is costly. If companies take the sink-or-swim approach, the cost — both to the bottom line and to employee morale — can be exorbitant as leaders go through the testing process. When an executive leaves a company, the cost to replace that person with someone from the outside can run into the hundreds of thousands, even millions of dollars. Fred Stuart of Stuart Recruiting estimates that the real cost of turnover is the equivalent of one year's pay. Hidden costs include the following:

■ Recruitment (when an outside recruiter is involved, this cost is typically one-third of the first year's pay)
■ Training replacements (which can negatively impact customer satisfaction)
■ Perception by shareholders of instability of the company
■ Reduced efficiency of those who work with a new recruit

Even the cost of slowly learning the job, vs. speeding the process through coaching, can have a significant impact on productivity.

Leaders are in high-visibility positions. When a job "doesn't work out," careers can be damaged and personal lives disrupted. People who feel that they were not successful because the job was misrepresented or that they did not have control of the resources they required for success often leave feeling bitter and angry. These feelings can carry over to future assignments and can have ongoing consequences. Senior executives have often given up secure positions elsewhere and uprooted their families to relocate. When it doesn't work out, it is not often easy to achieve previous levels of success.

Another false assumption that stops managers from coaching is the belief that academic success or intelligence is the best predictor of success in the workplace. This assumption is manifested when we see Fortune 500 companies hiring management trainees whom they have categorized as "the best and the brightest." For example, pharmaceutical companies typically recruit heavily from Ivy League schools and tell their newly minted graduates that they are being hired because they are the best. However, there is little correlation between success in school and success in the workplace.

The Case for Competencies

If academic and intellectual abilities are not predictors of success in the workplace, what are? The answer is competencies. Success at work has less to do with our intelligence than with how we handle ourselves with others, the initiative we take, and our ability to win support for our ideas. David McClelland, author of *Motives, Personality and Society,* was one of the first to make the case that behavioral competencies, rather than intelligence, was what differentiated successful people from their less successful peers in the workplace. He defined a *competency* as a personal characteristic, motive, behavior, skill, or knowledge that is proven to drive superior job performance.

McClelland, who is frequently credited as being the father of competencies, argued in the 1973 paper "Testing for Competence Rather than Intelligence" that traditional academic criteria, such as grades in school or academic aptitude, simply did not predict later success in the workplace. One of the easiest ways to show the relationship of the components of competencies is to picture an iceberg (see Figure 1.1).

Leaders typically flounder not because they lack the technical skills or knowledge to do the job, but rather because they have a competency deficit (for example, being unable to delegate or motivate others), which ultimately undermines their leadership.

Competency deficits — referred to as below the water line — are harder to see and harder to correct. So while acquiring a set of simple skills may only require taking relevant seminars or gleaning practical ideas from books, developing someone's motives, for example, is a difficult undertaking. Other behaviors or competencies that are below the water line include image, attitudes, and traits. They may not be readily apparent and are often difficult to measure. However, they are critically important, as they drive performance and are the key to performance results. Furthermore, these competencies are the most critical to leadership, a role whose essence is getting results through others. For example, interpersonal ineptitude in leaders lowers everyone's performance by wasting time, creating conflicts, lowering morale and commitment, and raising hostility and apathy. Competencies at the leadership level trickle down through the organization, positively impacting morale, motivation, commitment, and ultimately business results. How employees perceive their organizational culture is directly linked to the actions of the leaders.

More recently, the term *emotional intelligence* (EI) has created new interest in competency research and its applications in the business

What Are Competencies?

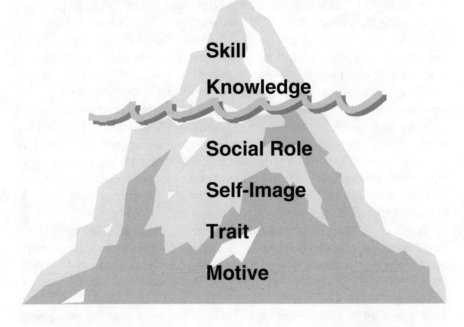

Skill

Knowledge

Social Role

Self-Image

Trait

Motive

Figure 1.1   The iceberg.

world. Daniel Goleman, who studied with David McClelland, has written several best-selling books that focus on a subset of competencies he has labeled as emotional intelligence, or those competencies that create the emotional fabric of an organization. The higher your level in an organization, the more important performance on competencies is to success on the job. Goleman argues, "For individuals in leadership positions, 85 percent of their competencies were in the EI domain."

Competencies — Popular but Underutilized

Many of the organizations I have worked with have already spent considerable time and resources developing specific competency models for their leadership teams. Yet despite all the research that has been done identifying the characteristics of outstanding leaders, when senior executives coach the leaders who work for them, do they effectively use the competency models in their coaching? Too often I see managers focusing their coaching on tactical problem-solving and only obliquely discussing the behavioral side of the problem or ignoring the competencies altogether. The focus of the conversation is on the attainment of goals, usually financial, without a full appreciation of how the behavioral side is instrumental in reaching and sustaining those targets.

Some companies have competency models that are never used, representing a waste of management and consultant time and company money. The models were either poorly understood or ineffectively implemented. In other cases, competencies were designed for a specific purpose, such as performance management or interviewing prospective new hires. If you have introduced competencies for a specific, narrowly defined purpose and are not using them for coaching, you have not maximized your investment.

Your company's leadership competency model may have been developed by a leadership team that is no longer with the company, or the business strategy may have changed over time. In these cases, your competency model may need to be revised; we discuss options for doing this in Chapter 5.

If you feel that you have good competency models in place, start using them. Have discussions with your executive team about what these competencies mean. For example, a leadership model often includes *communication* as a core competency. One of the communication behaviors for a leader might be to "communicate effectively down, up, and across the organization." This definition may mean one thing to you and something quite different to a leader you are coaching. Until you discuss how this competency applies in the unique situation each leader is dealing with, you don't have a dynamic definition of the competency that will be useful as a coaching tool.

Laying the foundation for coaching for competencies requires you to be willing to educate people about what the competencies mean to them and how the competencies are linked to business success in your organization. Teaching people requires more than a management presentation with PowerPoint slides. It requires telling stories, using examples, and making sure people understand how success is linked to performance in these competencies. It is an iterative process and requires that competencies be integrated into the discussion of business strategy on a regular basis. When your peers and direct reports see how you have taken the competencies seriously, they are more apt to incorporate the competencies into their daily thinking.

Competencies Can Be Learned

The key is that competencies can be learned and that coaching is the most effective strategy to ensure that new behavior is sustained over time. Competencies, or the lack of them, are behaviors that have grown into habits. Certain habits, such as poor listening and overreacting to stressful situations, are learned and are not easily changed. As Daniel Goleman points out in his book *Working With Emotional Intelligence,* developing competencies requires rewiring of the brain's circuitry; it is not a process that happens overnight or in a classroom session. The neocortex of our brain rapidly grasps concepts and comprehends new ideas. However, learning new behaviors and reeducation occur in the limbic brain. As Goleman puts it, "the limbic brain ... is a much slower learner, particularly when the challenge is to relearn deeply ingrained habits. The difference matters immensely when trying to improve leadership skills .... Reeducating the emotional brain for leadership learning ... requires a different model .... It needs lots of practice and repetition .... The task is doubled — we have to undo habits that do not work for us and replace them with new ones that do." Being aware that a competency deficiency is a problem is just the first step of the learning process. After awareness comes a lot of practice, course correction, more practice, support from others, and more practice. Because coaching is personal, goal-focused, and ongoing, it is ideally suited to providing the kind of support leaders need to build new skills and the habits required to sustain improved behaviors.

If you are a manager, you are in an ideal position to be a coach, because you are likely to see the leader in action and observe what he is doing.

A Case in Point ...

One leader I worked with needed to focus on making his communication more succinct. He had a tendency to ramble and digress, which created a significant obstacle to his impact on the organization. The more passionate he became about an issue, the more likely he was to talk at length — finally turning off his listener. I worked with him as an external coach while his manager coached him from an internal perspective. His manager was particularly effective at observing when this happened and gently reminded him of his commitment to be more direct and brief in making his point. It took several months for him to consistently change his behavior, but without coaching he never would have been able to unlearn the old habit and replace it with a newer, more effective one.

What Is Coaching and What Is Not?

When you are coaching, you have formed an explicit relationship with someone else to support him in personal and professional effectiveness. You are giving the person the gift of your presence to listen for understanding and to probe for empathy. As Warren G. Bennis, author of *Becoming a Leader,* has said, you have to be a "first-class noticer." You must be able to pay attention to the context and help the person you are coaching create meaning and perhaps see his or her experience in a new light. You don't have to be an expert in his area to do this. In fact, a good coach rarely gives advice but instead asks the right questions that help the person being coached get a fresh perspective on difficult issues.

You can be both a manager and a coach to the same individual, but be aware that these are two distinctly different roles. When you are operating with your managerial hat on, you have the organization's interests at heart. Your primary role is the responsibility to direct performance and ensure that the individual's efforts are aligned with the objectives of the organization. As a manager, you are responsible for holding others accountable for meeting their performance targets and for measuring the level of performance that was attained, as well as for the productivity of your organization.

As a coach, your responsibility is directed more toward the individual and to providing insight that will enable that leader to develop. In many respects, the coaching role is one of holding up a mirror so that the leader can more clearly see how he is impacting others. You are fostering self-insight and helping the leader grow through introspection and feedback from others. While these two roles are very different, a good manager should be effective at both. The power of being a manager who coaches is in the capacity to hold both of these perspectives as equally important.

Who Should Be Coaching?

All leaders need to be coaches and to build the bench strength of leadership of their organizations. As a manager, you are in a great position to coach, because who knows better than you what it really takes to be successful in your organization?

If you are in a senior management role, it's your responsibility to ensure that leadership is a source of vitality and productivity in your organization, focusing both on results and how those results are achieved. How leaders act is one of the single biggest levers of business results, and it is one of the few variables of business success over which you have direct influence. "Walking the talk" is about how a leader demonstrates the competencies that he is advocating for others. When a leader demonstrates competency strength, it is contagious; it impacts the entire organization and its customers, suppliers, and investors.

Using Internal Staff as Coaches

In addition to the role you must play in the coaching process, your internal staff, particularly in the human resource function, can be effective as partners in the coaching role. The role of human resources has been elevated over the past few decades from being focused on administrative responsibilities to becoming a full business partner. As the role has become more strategic, the human resource professional is often viewed as an advisor and internal consultant. Coaching and advising senior management is a key role for senior human resource staff to assume.

Hiring External Coaches

The role of the external executive coach has grown in popularity and usage in recent years, and it has received increased attention in the business community. The relationship of the executive coach, both to the client and to the organization for which he is doing the coaching, is critical for the process to be successful. Later in this book, I address the issues of when an external coach adds value to the leader and the organization, and what to look for when seeking the assistance of an external coach.

In your leadership coaching, it can be powerful to partner with an internal staff professional and an outside consultant. When I interviewed Beth Rubino, director of human resources development and training at QVC, she suggested that internal staff and external coaches should work together as a team. As she put it, "The partnership on my end offers the outside person an inside track on what is important to the business and how to align the work to other work that is going on in the company." All three coaching roles can be effective in developing leadership competencies. The purpose of this book is to help you understand how to optimize your approach to coaching, help you be a better coach of your own leaders, and clarify when and how to use professional coaches as an added asset in achieving business results.

How This Book Is Organized

The book is divided into three key sections, starting with a broad overview and moving into more specific applications of the coaching for competencies process. In Chapter 2, I address four key principles that are central to our approach to coaching for competencies and suggest what makes this type of coaching distinctive. Chapter 3 addresses competencies that you need to coach others.

The second section of the book is my perspective on corporate leadership and describes how to coach leaders to be effective. In Chapter 4, I describe the competencies that are most often identified with successful leaders and provide specific coaching tips for developing these competencies in your current leaders. For those who have not developed competency models or are looking to revise your approach in the future, Chapter 5 offers an overview of different strategies for developing competency models and the cost and benefits of each approach, particularly in relationship to coaching. The final chapter of the second section, Chapter 6, goes into depth about how to use 360-degree research as the foundation and catalyst of the coaching process. In this chapter, I show you what to look for when using a 360-degree feedback approach as a foundation for coaching and how to partner effectively with outside consultants to provide an objective perspective.

In the last section of the book, I explore coaching applications that you will most frequently encounter as a line manager. Chapter 7 reviews coaching on performance improvement, while Chapter 8 describes how to coach leaders' career development. In Chapter 9, I look at things that you need to be aware of when coaching people of different generations and how signals can get crossed when men and women are in a coaching relationship with each other. Finally, in Chapter 10, I offer suggestions on how to measure the effectiveness of your coaching initiative and how to ensure that coaching is occurring at all levels of your organization.

Throughout this book, I provide coaching tips and case studies that are designed to make you feel more capable in being an active coach and accelerate the learning and performance of those you work with.

Some of you are executives or human resource professionals who are attempting to be better coaches. Others are considering hiring an executive coach from outside your company. In preparation for this book we interviewed CEOs, senior corporate officers, and internal and external consultants who shared their perspectives with us. This book provides a framework for coaching others to achieve results. The text makes the business case that if you invest more time in the coaching process — your own time supported by additional coaching provided by others — you will see a measurable increase in the results you need through effective leadership of your organization.

This book is primarily written for line managers who want to be more effective coaches. However, at the senior level, executives often involve internal human resource professionals and/or outside executive coaches to provide additional coaching resources. An outside coach should never take the place of the coaching you need to do as a senior manager, but he can augment your coaching by providing a professional coach's perspective. This book helps you to identify when to use a professional coach and how to ensure that his coaching efforts are in alignment with your own.

References

1. Mitsch, D., *In Action: Coaching for Extraordinary Results,* ASTD, Alexandria, VA, 2003.
2. Anon., Executive coaching as a transfer of training tool: effects on productivity in a public agency, *Public Personnel Management,* Winter 1997, 26, 4, 461.
3. Goleman, D., Boyatzis R., and McKee, A., *Primal Leadership: Realizing the Power of Emotional Intelligence,* Harvard Business School Press, 2002.
4. Goleman, D., *Working with Emotional Intelligence,* Bantam Books, New York, 1998.
5. Bennis, W.G., *Becoming a Leader,* Perseus Publishing, New York, 1994.

Chapter 2

The Process of Coaching for Competencies

Who are the great coaches you have known in your lifetime? What made them great? Coaching is fundamentally a high-impact interaction. Coaches influence the beliefs and attitudes of the leaders they work with and help them expand their options when responding to difficult situations. The coach's role is to affect the leader's thinking and behavior in ways that may not only have broad-based business results but can be important to the leader's career for years to come.

Coaching, in general, is a process that requires commitment, honesty, diplomacy, and insight into human nature. Coaching for competencies is distinctive because it goes beyond helping someone solve an immediate problem. It is making a longer-term commitment to the development of that person's leadership potential. Specifically, coaching for competencies is *a process that fosters awareness and ongoing, sustained behavioral change, using data from multiple sources, that leads to enhanced business success.*

Why might this definition be useful? Several key parts are as follows:

- **A process** — Coaching is not just a single conversation or a scheduled meeting that is part of the performance-management process. It is a commitment that requires the coach to establish and maintain a relationship, over time, with the leader being coached.

- **That fosters awareness** — To improve performance on competencies, leaders must be able to see how their behavior impacts others in a new way. The coach can help the leader achieve this new level of awareness through direct observation, by sharing data on how the leader is seen by others, and by providing the leader with a forum for reflecting on alternative solutions to dilemmas.

- **Ongoing sustained behavioral change** — Achieving higher levels of performance requires not only pinpointing competencies on which to focus but also knowing what is required to maintain the new behavior over the long haul or in particularly challenging situations. Knowing what we can do better is not enough. Coaching helps leaders change their habits; these habits are the behavior patterns that can keep us from progressing.

- **Using data from multiple sources** — Coaching for competencies is unique in that it requires input from people who work closely with the leader. While the coach should rely on his own perceptions and reactions to what the leader is saying, the leader's own perceptions are only part of the picture. Coaching for competencies requires an integrated approach to collecting and analyzing data from multiple sources.

- **Leads to enhanced business success** — Coaching for competencies has a clear purpose. It is about helping leaders achieve results that are tied to their organization's goals. It is about creating a winning situation for everyone, promoting personal growth within the context of improving business results.

Coaching for competencies is a process that provides the lubricant for achieving business success. The coaching relationship has the potential for deepening an individual's understanding of his or her influence on the organization and for strengthening the personal commitment to achieving that organization's goals and outcomes.

Four Principles of Coaching for Competencies

Four basic principles are central to coaching for competencies. They permeate the entire coaching process and help the coach to meet the needs of both the leader and the organization. The first section of this chapter introduces you to the principles and how they work, while the second half outlines what you need as a coach (or what the coach you hire needs) to make these principles work. The four principles are as follows:

1. Clarify and make it explicit when you are coaching.
2. Use data-based feedback for personal development planning.
3. Frame competency issues in the context of a business problem.
4. Work toward ownership of the issues and a long-term commitment to competency improvement.

Principle One: Clarify and Make It Explicit When You Are Coaching

If you are a manager, you must make it clear when you are approaching a situation as a manager vs. when you are operating in the role of a coach. As a manager, you need to provide direction, set expectations for performance, and ultimately evaluate the results. The role of the manager must come first. If direction hasn't been clearly set, coaching is not useful. However, when you are in the role of a coach, the focus is less on evaluation and more on learning.

A coach's job is essentially to provide different perspectives or viewpoints by listening, observing, and then intervening to heighten awareness concerning issues about which the individual might have been previously or partially unaware. A coach provides a leader with a variety of ways to think about a given situation. This opens the way for the leader being coached to make choices about changing behavior and about what steps should be taken next. As a manager, you often need to quickly intervene and make decisions to redirect or strongly influence a business decision. When this occurs, you have your management hat on. While the leader with whom you are working may learn a great deal in the resolution of the current problem, this approach should not be confused with coaching for competencies where you are more focused on the longer-term development of the person you are coaching.

Principle Two: Use Data-Based Feedback for Personal Development Planning

Unlike other approaches to competencies, coaching for competencies is a data-based process that typically includes a multisource assessment (also known as 360-degree feedback) in the early stages of the coaching relationship. This means that you need to gather information about the person being coached from a variety of sources — not just from the person's supervisor, but from his colleagues, teammates, direct reports, and even his customers (if appropriate). The reason for this is key to understanding coaching for competencies: what is critical in business relationships is not the leader's intent but the impact he has on others.

The intent of our behavior is one thing, but the impact of our behavior can be quite different. Even a manager who berates his employees does not necessarily intend to be mean; he acts in a way that he believes will have positive results.

Using multisource feedback as the foundation of the coaching process gives greater validity and depth to the coach's perceptions of the leader. It also makes the coach's recommendations more compelling. Most senior executives are comfortable using data to solve business issues. They are more convinced when they "see the numbers." Getting feedback that is grounded in a solid data-gathering process can help them understand and accept their areas of strength as well as the areas that need development.

With data-based feedback, leaders can become aware of how others are reading their behavior and can choose to change their behavior to enhance success and opportunities in the organization.

Principle Three: Frame Competency Issues in the Context of a Business Problem

Coaching for competencies is really about encouraging the leaders who work for you to reflect and change their behavior. Executives are not always initially comfortable looking at how their own behavior can contribute to a business problem. After all, most leaders have already achieved a level of success and like to view themselves as smart, capable, and effective. In fact, a large measure of what has led them to the position of responsibility has been their success in getting results. So when a coach approaches a leader for the first time, it is understandable that the leader may have doubts about spending time discussing "competencies" that will have value on business results.

A leader can become more comfortable dealing with a behavioral issue when it is connected to the business results that he or she is trying to achieve. The coach's role is to get the leader to see the integral connection between the two (see Figure 2.1).

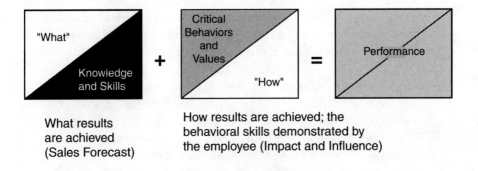

What results
are achieved
(Sales Forecast)

How results are achieved; the
behavioral skills demonstrated by
the employee (Impact and Influence)

Figure 2.1 Two aspects of performance. Planning in both areas is necessary for effective performance.

A Case in Point ...

Sandra had worked as a vice president of a Fortune 500 international telecommunications company for a number of years prior to taking a job with a midsize company that was still in a high-growth mode. She was welcomed into the firm because she brought knowledge and contacts that she had accumulated through her years of experience at the Fortune 500 company. In her new job, she joined a small management team that was used to consulting each other on key decisions — they did not have the same formal infrastructure of communication that Sandra had come to rely on in her prior position.

After the first few months in her new position, Sandra began to run into trouble. Wanting to get quick business results, she tended to ramrod her proposals forward without consulting her colleagues. Executive team meetings were rarely held, and when they were, Sandra argued vigorously for approval of her agenda without regard for the competing needs of her colleagues. Other executives felt that she was abrasive and adversarial. Sandra was frustrated that the company was moving so slowly on funding the proposals that she felt she had been hired to implement.

Sandra's boss realized that the situation needed an executive coach with an objective perspective and asked if I would be willing to be a coach for Sandra. My initial challenge was to understand Sandra's perspective on the situation, so the first session was spent allowing Sandra to vent some of her feelings. Then my job was to help Sandra see the situation from a fresh perspective. Because of her experience in a large company, where she needed to fight for attention, she came into the smaller company like a bull in a china shop. When she described her current dilemma to me, she didn't seem to be aware that she was sabotaging herself by how she treated others. She needed to gain greater awareness of the impact of her behavior and realize that unless she was willing to change how she acted, the business and personal consequences would likely be disastrous. Helping Sandra connect the dots both defused the emotions of the situation and created the business context for us to explore the issues in more depth in subsequent sessions.

Principle Four: Work toward Ownership of the Issues and a Long-Term Commitment to Competency Improvement

The fourth principle of the coaching process is to be sure that the person being coached is committed to the process and is willing to look at how she may be creating or contributing to a difficult situation. If the leader does not see the need for change, there is no motivation — and therefore no learning. Commitment to participation in the discovery process is essential for change. Therefore, if you are a manager and either want to assume a coaching role or want to bring in an outside executive coach, you must first get the leader to understand why you believe in coaching and ensure that the leader perceives this as positive support. Share your own experiences of being coached or of people who have coached you and the difference it made to your success. Coaching imposed from above, without first preparing the groundwork, is often resented and fails to be effective for the person who needs to change.

What Do You Need to Be a Great Coach?

Many competencies can make coaches effective; some are obvious. If you were the one being coached, you would want someone who was a thoughtful listener and who seemed to care about you and your concerns. Coaching for competencies requires the same patience and communication skills that are required for all helping relationships. But coaching for competencies also lends itself to a particular skill set that is organized around the four principles previously discussed. Whether you are doing the coaching yourself or are hiring an external executive coach to assist in the process, you should assess whether the coach can effectively demonstrate these competencies.

Putting Principle One into Effect: Clarify and Make It Explicit When You Are Coaching

If you are planning to coach someone who works for you to develop that person's leadership competencies, he or she is going to look to you as a role model for the behaviors you are addressing. As a coach, you must have enough maturity to understand how your own strengths and weaknesses appear to others and what you can bring to the coaching engagement. That is why self-awareness and openly sharing perceptions and experiences are the cornerstones of coaching for competencies.

Self-Awareness

Self-awareness means understanding who I am and how my own background and experiences have shaped my values and perspectives on life. Coaching is fundamentally a relationship. As in all relationships, how we see ourselves and how much we understand ourselves shape the nature of the relationships we create. Self-awareness means that the coach can use himself as an instrument to connect with the leader and to get a sense of the issues at hand.

The coach's first job is to expand the leader's self-awareness so that the leader can have a more realistic view of his strengths and weaknesses. This enables the person to build a repertoire of behavioral responses to difficult situations in the workplace. As a coach, how you act and react to the leaders you are coaching sends a more powerful message than what you say. A lack of self-awareness can undermine your credibility, regardless of the business skills you bring to the table as a coach.

Coaching Tips ...

Self-awareness goes beyond how you are feeling at the moment and extends to being aware of how you impact others. How you act and react enhances the probability that you are connecting on an emotional and intellectual level with the leader. This connection allows you to be influential in your coaching and to serve as an effective role model for the leader in the process.

The more self-aware you are, the more you can use yourself as an instrument of coaching. Self-awareness provides valuable clues as to whether the match between you and the leader is a good one.

Dorothy E. Siminovitch, Ph.D., co-chair and faculty of the Gestalt Institute of Cleveland's International Coaching Program, explains that there are two critical orientation issues to keep in mind as an executive coach. At the beginning of a coaching relationship, it is imperative to determine why the leader is asking for coaching and what the leader's goals are. Second, as an executive coach it is important to know if you have the skill set and knowledge base to help the leader meet those goals.

"If a leader came to me for help in solving a physics problem, the decision is clear. I would decline because I do not have the appropriate skill set and knowledge base for this issue," says Siminovitch. "So, when I meet a new leader, I determine if I have the repertoire and knowledge base to enable me to join the leader in pursuit of his or her goals. It is the development work of the coach to determine if she has the skills and knowledge to understand how factors like human development and personality, motivation, resistance, and theories for change will affect the work in coaching. It is the coach's task to determine that she carries the relevant skills and knowledge to assist the client in pursuit of his or her goals. It is the coach's ethical duty to engage in self-awareness and self-evaluation in service of what she can bring to the client's learning."

Openly Share Perceptions and Experiences

Making every coaching session count requires more than self-awareness. It also requires that when you are acting as a coach, you are willing to openly share perceptions and experiences directly with the leader. This is key to building a trusting relationship. No one is open to advice or feedback from someone they don't like or respect. A coach must be willing and able to authentically relate his or her feelings and reactions to what is happening with the leader. This is known as *being authentic*. As Peter Block writes in his landmark book *Flawless Consulting*, being authentic "means that you put into words what you are experiencing with the leader as you work." This is one of the most powerful things you can do to influence the leader. Leaders are more willing to disclose how they feel with someone who is being authentic with them.

Coaching Tips ...

Remember, a coach is not a therapist. (Therapists rarely share their own experiences with clients.) If you are touched by what the leader is saying or have shared a similar experience that would shed light on the situation, it's usually a good idea to express those thoughts to the leader. For example, if a leader is nervous about making her first major presentation, you might share a story about how nervous you were in a similar situation, and how you were able to get past your nerves and up to the podium.

If a leader has called you in as a coach, she wants to know that you have the ability and commitment to be of help. In many cases, the leader has been trying to resolve the troubling issue(s) and has gotten stuck. She wants to believe that involving you will help her get to where she wants to go. That means sharing your relevant background, prior experience, and expertise to reassure her that you have successfully helped others who have experienced the same or similar difficulties.

Being authentic can also involve expressing negative thoughts and reactions. If something in your interaction is making you uncomfortable, you should be honest and let the leader know about it — as long as you do so in a way that is not hurtful or destructive. You can be honest without being blunt. Being blunt means that you say what you feel with no regard as to how it is going to impact the other person. Being honest, or authentic, means expressing how you feel (even if it causes discomfort) in a tactful, diplomatic manner.

When a coach openly shares perceptions and experiences, it helps the leader believe that the coach is genuine and does not have a hidden agenda. The successful coach is able to assure the leader that he genuinely cares about his success and that his advice, judgments, and decisions are based on the leader's best interests, rather than his own. Once the bond of integrity is broken it is difficult, if not impossible, to repair. If a leader feels that the coach's advice is politically motivated or is in some way in the coach's self-interest, the bond of trust will be irreparably broken.

Putting Principle Two into Effect: Use Data-Based Feedback for Personal Development Planning

One of the distinguishing principles of coaching for competencies is that it is based on data that can come from a variety of sources, including 360-degree surveys, interviews, and the coach's own observations of the leader. Due to the data-driven nature of the coaching, two of the critical coaching competencies are (a) the coach's ability to listen for understanding and (b) understanding and managing the data from numerous sources.

Listening for Understanding: Asking Behavioral Event Questions

Data gathering almost always involves interviewing the leader and those who work closely with him. Asking perceptive questions and probing for specific examples enable the coach to fully understand how the leader understands his situation, the logic he applies to the problems he is facing, and his capacity to be sensitive to the emotional dimensions of the people around him.

Behavioral event interviewing is a technique that is particularly useful in a coaching situation. It is a strategy used to elicit underlying feelings and thoughts that reveal someone's motivation and fundamental competencies in critical situations. Specific questions directed to particular competencies can be combined with the 360-degree feedback survey data to reveal powerful elements regarding a leader's capabilities.

Coaching Tips ...

A key component of a behavioral-based interview is asking a leader to be specific about her own experiences, behaviors, and goals. For instance, if you are coaching a leader who is having difficulty dealing effectively with a poor performer who reports to her, you may want to spend some time understanding the underlying dynamics between the leader you are coaching and the direct report (who has the performance problem). The following questions are typical:

■ What creates difficulties for you in communicating with this person?

- What did you do to plan for a meeting with the direct report?
- When you get frustrated with your direct report, what do you say?
- If you experience resistance, what do you do?
- What were you thinking at the time?

These are examples of the type of coaching questions that allow you to recognize the underlying issues in the situation. Getting the leader to be as specific as possible is critical to the coaching process. It not only helps you understand what the leader wants and needs, but it also allows the leader to reflect on her own reactions to complex situations. This type of guided reflection is often the first step toward expanded self-awareness.

Asking good questions also involves listening carefully and hearing the leader's needs, aspirations, anxieties, and conflicts. Focusing your attention on what the leader is saying requires you to suspend your own thoughts, judgments, and reactions and instead concentrate on where the leader is going in the conversation. We all have a tendency to edit what someone else is saying. For example, a manager might be telling you about how his employees are not coming to him early enough when there is a sign of a problem, and you immediately start thinking about how you would fix the problem if you were this manager. You are putting your emotional and intellectual energy into mentally fixing the problem, rather than listening for its underlying symptoms; for example, why there is a disconnection between this manager and his employees or what this manager may be doing to exacerbate the problem. You build trust and optimize the opportunity to find longer-term solutions when you focus on the problem from the leader's point of view.

Understanding and Managing the Data

An effective coach is able to gather a wide variety of opinions and perspectives, and can integrate them into a coherent framework that the leader can understand and use to make decisions about what to do next.

An expert, either a trained human resource professional or an outside executive coach, can often be a resource to implement an in-depth 360-degree feedback analysis; we discuss this in more detail in Chapter 6. As the manager of someone receiving this type of feedback, you don't want the leader to become overwhelmed by receiving a "data dump." If you are a manager, you need to be knowledgeable about the dynamics of the process, how the data are analyzed, and how to distill the information from the multirater feedback into a few key areas in which the leader can take action.

Confidentiality: The Cornerstone of Trust

One of the problems that coaches face is maintaining confidentiality of the data collected. This is the cornerstone of building trust, yet in many situations, this is more difficult than it initially appears — for both internal and external coaches. The person who brings an external coach into an organization (and pays the bills) is often not the person being coached. Internal coaches are often assigned by upper management. When management brings in a coach for Sue or Harry, these managers have a right to check on the progress that is being made. In these situations, trust must be built — with both the leader being coached and with management who has requested the coaching.

To avoid problems, the coach must take the time to understand what both the leader and his supervisor expect from the process. Alignment of goals between the leader and the organization should occur early in the coaching process. As in any business arrangement, management should know how progress toward the stated goals is to be measured. This gets especially complex when a coach is asked by senior management to coach other leaders in the organization. In this case, there are two leaders with two different sets of needs: senior management, who has engaged the coach in the assignment, and the leader with whom the coach is working. To build a trusting relationship with the leader who is being coached, it is essential to establish from the start who gets to see any data that are collected or reports that are written. Clarifying up-front what information the coach has to share with management versus what information is confidential to the leader is critical to ongoing success.

A Case in Point ...

> Renee Booth, a leading executive coach and president of Leadership Solutions, often coaches several people within the same company, which sometimes puts her in a precarious position. "These people are interacting on a daily basis," she says. "And at the same time, they're telling you their secrets. When I first started consulting, I wasn't sure how to handle this kind of situation. What I learned is that from the beginning, you have to let everybody understand your position about keeping those secrets. They must understand that the point of having all this information is to be able to use it to help them fix a problem or sticky situation. So at some point, they have to trust your judgment about what you will say and what you will not say.

> "I worked in one company where two men were competing for the same job. I knew all about each of them, what their fears were, what their strengths were, what their weakness were. They both knew that I had this information about each of them, and became really anxious when they saw me in the hall with the other one. The only way to deal with it was to be straight with them, to be authentic. I had to tell one that he probably wasn't going to get the job. It was actually a relief to him to know that the decision had been made. We talked about what that would mean to him and what his options were. It was the only way to defuse the tension in the company and to help the leader make a smooth transition into the next phase of his life and career."

Putting Principle Three into Effect: Frame Competency Issues in the Context of a Business Problem

Coaching in a business environment should be driven by mutually agreed-upon goals that focus on personal or managerial effectiveness in the service of business performance. The coach serves as a resource for development activities, but more importantly, serves to connect the perceptions of the leader's strengths and development goals with specific business results. For example, a leader may need to work on interpersonal effectiveness, both inside and outside the workplace. However, it is most effective to use this as a coaching goal if both the coach and the leader understand the impact of this behavior on the business.

It is often not immediately apparent to leaders how changing their behavior can impact the financial performance of the organization. This is especially true when a leader has been able to achieve a good track record of results, despite some behavioral problems. The coach who helps a leader understand the connection between changing behavior and manifesting different or better results can help that leader build a commitment to action.

Reframing: The Art of Offering a Fresh Perspective

An old saying is "If you do what you've always done, you get what you've always gotten." People often find themselves stuck because they try the same actions repeatedly and, not surprisingly, get the same results. They end up in a nonproductive pattern that keeps producing the opposite results from what they want. For example, a sales manager who wants his team to meet its quota may try berating his salespeople to motivate them. When they still don't meet the quota, he berates them even more. The manager is soon stuck in this behavior, even though it is lowering morale and taking him farther away from the numbers he needs. The diagnostic skills that the coach brings should help the leader get unstuck, help him to move forward and take action, and provide a fresh perspective that motivates the leader to try something new.

Many leaders get a coach only after they have tried and failed to solve a problem on their own. For the most part, the leader has a perspective on what is not going well. Unfortunately, the strategies that the leader has been using to resolve the issue have not produced the results that he or she (or the organization) are looking for.

Listening carefully to the leader's perspective on the situation and acknowledging the validity and uniqueness of the problem are critical steps to building a foundation for reframing the problem. Leaders are much more likely to be open to the coach's perspective once they feel that their points of view have also been understood. Furthermore, using data collected in a multisource approach can be a powerful tool for helping the leader to recognize important discrepancies between how he sees himself and how he is seen by others.

A Case in Point ...

Jack was a leader who received multirater feedback that suggested some of his direct reports found him difficult to trust. His reports didn't believe he was genuinely interested in their welfare. When we gave Jack this feedback, he was dismayed but not surprised. He believed that this situation originated not because of anything that he was doing but because he had been sent from the corporate office. He thought he was viewed as an outsider who had been brought in to reorganize the division. He believed that the negative feedback was coming from several employees who had been with the company for many years before it was acquired by the larger corporation. Because the company had a strong policy of not terminating long-time employees, he could not fire them, but he felt that they would never accept him as part of their team.

We helped Jack reframe the problem by getting him to understand why these employees harbored resentment toward him. We wanted him to see himself from their per-spective, whether he agreed with their assessment or not. He needed to understand that they felt threatened and under-valued for their prior accomplishments. The feedback from these employees was that Jack conveyed a sense of coolness and superiority that the employees found off-putting. This was compounded by their feelings that someone within their group should have been appointed head of the department.

We also challenged Jack to think through the real cost of letting this problem linger in contrast to the benefits of improving teamwork with these employees. We asked him to think of the implications in broader terms beyond his immediate team, including how the rest of the organization would perceive him.

We helped Jack reframe his thinking to understand that changing his behavior could help others see him as a more supportive leader and that this would make a difference in morale, and ultimately, in performance.

Putting Principle Four into Effect: Work toward Ownership of the Issues and a Long-Term Commitment to Competency Improvement

One of the most powerful things you can do as a coach is help leaders believe in themselves and help them realize that they are capable of more than they ever thought possible. This can release energy that may be lying dormant underneath the apprehensiveness the leader may be feel about facing the unknown or untried. As a coach, showing your own confidence in the leader can create excitement about future possibilities. Coaching, at its best, can provide a sense of hope, and hope energizes action. The leader needs to feel genuinely optimistic that problems can be solved.

Motivation comes from within, but the effective coach can discover what uniquely motivates each leader and help him feel excited about his journey. This is achieved by reaching people intellectually, but it also taps into their emotions so that they are motivated not only to take action but to make change a priority. People are motivated in many ways. Knowing the leader you are coaching on a deeper level and tapping into his unique values and aspirations can trigger those factors that compel him or her to go beyond awareness and to take action.

Using the coaching competencies we discussed earlier, especially listening at a deeper level, and openly sharing your own perceptions and experiences, you can provide a foundation for authentic encouragement and reassurance to move forward.

A Case in Point …

Barbara is a vice president of human resources of a regional bank and has been in the field for more than 30 years. She is bright and knowledgeable, and is able to infuse the organization with her own sense of humor and compassion. Barbara's interest in the arts has always been a strong avocation. However, in the past several years, she has grown weary of driving the changes that are required in the new competitive banking environment, and her sense of enthusiasm for the work has declined.

Barbara called me for some coaching, as she was considering taking an early retirement from her organization to pursue her artistic interests. But she did not feel ready, financially or emotionally, to end her banking career. She saw the early retirement as more of a sabbatical to rethink her longer-term career choices. She was concerned that if she left the workforce for a year, it would be difficult to come back.

It was important to reassure Barbara of her professional value and worth, and to coach her on how to leave without burning bridges. During the process, I was able to share my own personal experience in making major professional changes. This not only strengthened our bond, but it allowed her to gain more confidence to make her decision to leave her job and feel that doors were opening, not shutting behind her.

Dealing with Resistance

The road to long-term competency development and improving performance is rarely a smooth one. Leaders typically welcome coaching when it is viewed as support for developing their careers. In this situation, leaders are usually open to feedback. However, a leader may feel less comfortable if he thinks that he is being coached because of perceived problems with his performance. The leader may not agree with management's assessment, or he may feel negatively judged or subtly coerced by the organization to accept coaching. That's the first instance when resistance is most likely to occur. The second time you are likely to run into resistance is when the leader receives specific feedback with which he either disagrees or is not ready to hear.

Resistance is a natural part of the coaching situation — as it is with most situations in life that require change. We all have a tendency to resist what is new, especially if the change is initiated by someone else. As Peter Block states in *Flawless Consulting,* "The important thing to understand about resistance is that it is a reaction to an emotional process taking place within the client."

Most leaders are looking for a coach who can help them gain greater clarity on important issues so that they can make better business decisions or solve difficult problems. They want to take effective actions that produce successful results. Even so, they may exhibit resistance without realizing it. Frequently, resistant behavior makes sense on the surface, but it only serves to delay making decisions or taking action. It is a common emotional response to being faced with a difficult organizational problem.

Resistance can be expressed in a variety of ways, including intellectualizing, asking for more detail than is necessary in a situation, procrastinating on the action plan, or passively agreeing with the coach but taking no action.

However, the most common form of resistance, and the one that most often holds leaders back from developing their competencies to the fullest extent, is the statement "I'm not the problem; *they* are." Blaming others deflects the need for a leader to reflect on how his own actions have created the problem he is now facing.

A Case in Point ...

When you encounter resistance, the best thing you can do is express to your client how you are sizing up the situation at the moment. Naming the resistance you are experiencing in everyday language and in a neutral, non-confrontational tone can be a powerful intervention in the relationship with the leader you are coaching, because it allows that person to make a more direct statement about his or her underlying concerns. When someone is given the opportunity to think through and articulate his objections, the energy often goes out of the resistance and the leader is able to move forward.

For example, I was recently called in to work with an executive team to provide 360-degree feedback and coaching for each team member. The senior vice president of information technology explained that she was in total support of the initiative but was overwhelmed with time commitments; she didn't know if she could fit this into her other priorities. When I was finally able to sit down with her, she seemed confused about the process and had not taken the initial steps required to trigger the data gathering. I didn't pressure her in this meeting but reiterated the objectives of the project and asked her whether she had any concerns about participating.

In talking through the process, I gave her the opportunity to get to know me and to determine whether she felt the coaching process could be helpful. I also expressed, in a positive but neutral way, that it would be her decision, in conjunction with that of her boss, whether we would move ahead. The next day, she told me she was ready to get started with the process. By addressing her resistance directly, I allowed her to identify her underlying concern and move toward action. The dialogue between us went something like this:

Coach: It has been difficult to reach you to schedule this meeting. I know you are busy, but I was wondering if you were reluctant to participate in this process. Do you have any concerns?

Leader: I know this is important, and I believe in this sort of thing. It is just that I'm so busy, and I don't know how this should fit into my other responsibilities. I don't know if my boss thinks this should be a priority.

Coach: If time is the issue, why don't you talk this over with your boss and get back to me with your decision tomorrow.

Sometimes the resistance is more subtle. You may be coaching someone who at first appears relieved to have someone to whom he can freely vent his frustrations. The fact that the person you are coaching can appear open and engaged may still be a form of resistance if he isn't taking responsibility for his role in the situation and therefore is unwilling to look at what he needs to do to change. The following are examples of how this attitude manifests itself:

■ The leader who can't motivate her team and blames it on team members whom she inherited from her predecessor. She says, "If I only could replace these people, we would be more successful."

■ The leader who feels that unrealistic demands are being made by corporate headquarters. He says, "They don't really understand our business and the pressures we are under from our competition."

- The leader who can't get the cooperation and resources that are needed from another department. He says, "We would have the contracts done on time if they weren't being held up in the legal department."

In all of these examples, the leader appears to have good explanations for why his performance is suffering. However, the source of the problem always seems to be outside of his control. In essence, the leader sees himself as a victim of circumstances and can therefore avoid moving forward to make the necessary changes.

This is often the starting point of a coaching engagement. The power of the 360-degree feedback data is that they enable the leader to gain a broader awareness of his role and the impact he has on others through quantifiable numbers as well as through findings from interviews. If, even after seeing these data, the leader still insists that the problem is caused by other people, you can be sure that resistance is the issue.

Regardless of the form of the resistance, by helping the person you are coaching express it directly, you help him move forward and use what the coach has to offer. If someone isn't taking responsibility for his role in a difficult situation, as a coach you might simply say, "You don't seem to see yourself as part of this situation." The art of moving people out of their resistance and into action involves carefully observing what they are doing, understanding their motivation, and finally pointing out behaviors that are counterproductive. When coaching for competencies, it is critical to ask the leader to reflect on the business implications of holding onto his belief-limiting views of the situation.

Coaching for competencies rests on the competencies of the coach. It is often not immediately apparent to leaders how a change in their behavior can impact the performance of the organization. This is especially true when an executive has been able to achieve a good track record of results despite some behavioral problems. The coach who can be empathetic and at the same time use data to help the leader understand the connection between changing behavior and manifesting different or better results can help the leader build a stronger leadership style and ultimately a more productive organization.

Reference

1. Block, P., *Flawless Consulting: A Guide to Getting Your Expertise Used,* Jossey-Bass, San Francisco, CA, 1999.

Chapter 3

The Coaching Process

Many managers I work with get so busy meeting deadlines, going to meetings, or just getting the work done, they feel that they don't have much time left to coach. Others are physically separated from the people who report to them, whether they are on a different floor of the same office building or in a different part of the world. In our fast-paced world, if you are truly committed to the development of your people, you must go out of your way to make yourself accessible to them.

We discuss two kinds of coaching in this chapter. The first is a spontaneous opportunity that I call a "coachable moment." It is really a snapshot approach; it is seizing opportunities as you find them and capitalizing on experiences as learning opportunities.

The second type of coaching is a longer-term approach that requires planning and follow-up. While this greater level of investment on both the part of the coach and that of the person being coached is focused on producing deeper, longer-lasting, deeper-competency development, the two approaches are not mutually exclusive. As a manager, you can assist people in their development by using both approaches. One coaching style does not take the place of the other, and both can support development of leadership competencies.

The Coachable Moment

Opportunities for coaching can occur in the context of everyday events. A coachable moment is an impromptu opportunity for learning that occurs in the context of solving a business issue.

A Case in Point ...

Gail might be discussing a proposed staffing change to the organization with one of her managers, Edward. While discussing strategy, Edward mentions that he is having difficulty interacting with one of his direct reports. Gail sees this as a coachable moment and instead of immediately offering her opinion says, "Tell me a little bit more about the situation." At that moment, the focus of the interaction shifts from the proposed organizational change to Edward and his personal experience of working with his direct report. After discussing the situation for a few minutes, Edward might directly ask Gail for advice and support. Or, Gail might take the initiative and offer a new perspective to help Edward clarify his next steps in dealing with his direct report. That's a coachable moment. There is no formal contract and no time spent beyond the 10 or 20 minutes of exploration, but at the end Edward feels heard, recognized, and assisted with a situation that was causing him some difficulty.

The opportunity to coach others or to be coached ourselves occurs all the time; we just don't always label it as such. Many of us experience these coachable moments as we go through the day. We often find ourselves asking for support, a different perspective, and a second viewpoint. We experience such moments with our friends, coworkers, children, and spouses, and afterward we generally feel that our own lives have been enriched.

Coachable moments must be seized when they appear, because they are extremely valuable. Take advantage of a request for assistance. It's a way to connect and to build relationships. Most importantly, these moments often help people grow and develop to a greater extent than they would from a stiffer or more formal interaction. This is the time when the person asking for help is most open to hearing a different perspective.

A second type of coachable moment occurs when we observe a leader in action and see him either exercising new competency skills or slipping back into old habits. We already discussed how learning new competencies is a process that occurs over time. Competency development requires breaking old habits and replacing them with new ones. As with any other habit, we typically regress into old patterns at times. When you are coaching a leader who is developing a specific competency, start a coaching dialogue as soon after a critical incident as possible. The immediacy of the dialogue and feedback can have a significant impact on sustaining competency development and can continue a positive momentum to sustained behavioral change.

Coaching Tips ...

The following points can help you recognize a coachable moment:

- Did you just see the leader in action where the targeted competency was called for? What happened regarding the targeted behaviors?
- Is the leader motivated to reflect and learn about how his behavior is contributing to the results?
- Is the timing right?

As a manager, remember that a coachable moment is not the time for a mini performance review. The leader being coached is all too aware that you are his manager. If the leader feels he is being evaluated rather than helped, his defenses will go up, and the opportunity for deeper learning that can contribute to competency development will be lost. Instead, ask reflective questions and probe for deeper understanding of the situation.

Coaching for Sustained Behavioral Change

While coachable moments can be a significant part of a strategy for longer-term development, this is usually not enough. Competency development requires the same rigorous approach of planning and consistent follow-up that are typically applied to other business processes.

Five Steps of Coaching for Competencies

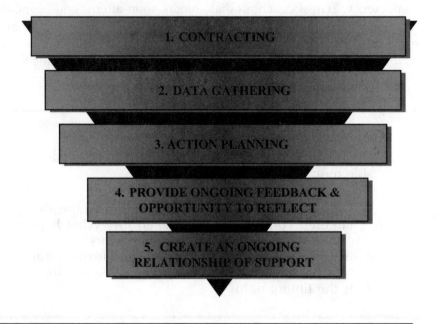

Figure 3.1   Five steps of coaching for competencies.

Our coaching model is an ongoing process with five key steps (see Figure 3.1).

Step One: Contracting for Coaching

Be a Manager First and a Coach Second

If you are a manager, be clear that the role of the manager and that of the coach are not the same. As a manager, your job is to establish goals and performance expectations. As a coach, your role is to help leaders develop the management skills they need to accomplish those results. These are two separate and sequential tasks that a boss needs to do. The job of the manager comes first. If someone who works for you is not clear about the organizational goals or specific competency expectations, coaching will be a waste of time.

Clarify which issues you want to address with your management hat on and which issues you are amenable to coaching. As a manager, some situations require you to correct mistakes or evaluate someone else's performance. When you are trying to redirect poor performance, you are probably focusing more on controlling the situation than on making it a learning opportunity for the leader. You are acting appropriately as a manager, but don't confuse this with being a coach.

Fit between the Coach and the Leader

Once you have made it explicit that you are acting as a coach, the initial sessions provide a time for the coach and the leader to size up the situation. Questions are being asked on both sides, whether they are articulated or are only internal musings. Both parties are trying to determine the degree of fit in the relationship. Not all people are a good match for each other. This is true if you are a coaching manager or an outside executive coach. The first meeting gives the leader being coached a chance to ask herself these types of questions:

- Can I work with this coach?
- Does he understand my issues?
- Can he see the problem from my point of view?
- Do I think I can learn from him and be motivated by what he has to say?

At the same time, if you are a coach, you should be scanning your own experience and reflecting on these types of questions:

- Is this person willing to reflect on the part she is playing?
- What do I have to offer this person within the situation we are discussing?
- Is this person open to change?

The fit between the coach and the person being coached must be a good one. As Mary Beth O'Neill states in *Executive Coaching with Backbone and Heart,* "In many ways, contracting is the most important phase. Both people — coach and leader — build a relationship and establish credibility .... Together they need to draw the goals and parameters for the coaching relationship and set up expectations that drive the rest of the phases."

The goal of contracting is to clarify what the leader wants and what the coach can provide. As a coach, explore the issues facing the leader and see if they fit a coaching approach. Contracting for coaching means that you are making an explicit agreement with someone to offer long-term support and to be a role model for leadership. Don't be afraid to share what you can offer as a coach. At times, managers are apprehensive about taking this step for fear that they will say the wrong thing or that their desire to help will be misinterpreted as a sign of weakness.

The goal of the first step of the coaching process is to agree to periodically step back and exchange ideas and insights on what both the coach and the leader are learning to adapt to new demands and challenges. It is the initial opportunity the coach has to link what the individual wants to happen with what the organization expects. What are the leader's own perceptions of the competencies required to get the job done? What initial insight does she have into her own style and that of the people she works with? Coaching needs to frame competency issues in the context of what the organization is trying to achieve.

When problems arise, a natural tendency is to intensify our efforts but essentially do more of the same, even if it isn't working. Leaders, like all of us, can regress to old patterns of behavior. Coaching offers the opportunity to take a timeout and ask the leader to reflect on the situation and understand how his pattern of behavior is perpetuating the problem rather than resolving it. With an increased sense of self-awareness that comes from coaching, leaders can begin to let go of limiting behavior and test the competencies that may be better suited to the situation.

Get to Know the Leader on a Deeper Level

During the initial stage, it is important for you to get to know the leader you are coaching at a deeper level. Only by understanding her view of the world, the assumptions she holds, and the values she cherishes will you have a deeper understanding of what is truly important to that individual and what motivates her to action. In their book *Primal Leadership,* Daniel Goleman, Richard Boyatzis, and Anne McKee cite definitive research that suggests that people are only motivated to change their behavior for the long haul when they see how it links to who they are as a person — beyond the organization they are working in and the job they are doing. It means understanding what their hopes and dreams are, what creates excitement for them, and what future they want to create for themselves.

Agree on What the Coaching Process Will Look Like

At the conclusion of the contracting discussion, both the leader and the coach should have a feel for the playing field: the issues the leader wants to explore, the process the coach will follow for organizing the coaching engagement, and an initial impression of being in a relationship with each other. Decide how often you will meet, whether your sessions will be in person or on the telephone, how you will incorporate feedback from other people, and whether the coach will have the opportunity to observe the leader in action. These items should all be discussed up front.

The Value of Revisiting the Contract

Contracting occurs within the first meeting between the coach and the leader. It reoccurs within each subsequent meeting to clarify the goal of that specific coaching session. This contracting can be as simple and informal as asking the following questions:

- What would you like to focus on in this session?
- How can I help you today?
- Based upon our earlier discussion, how does this fit into your overall goal?

The purpose of these microcontracting discussions is to ensure that the relationship between coach and leader remains healthy and relevant to the needs of the leader. It allows both people to redefine the situation based upon what has happened since their last meeting, and it ensures that the discussion is owned by both parties.

Step Two: Gathering the Data

Once the coaching relationship is established, the coach and the leader need to talk to others who can provide additional perspectives on the leader's impact on the organization. If you are a coaching manager, you will undoubtedly have your own point of view of the leader's strengths and shortcomings. However, even if you can observe this leader in action on a regular basis, you are still seeing only one angle of the situation. How the leader sees himself is another important snapshot. Other pictures from his direct reports, peers, and even customers might look quite different. That is why a multirater approach, taken from a variety of angles, provides the most valuable way to construct a picture of the leader's competency strengths and weaknesses.

Numbers Tell the Story

The key purpose of collecting data is to expand the leader's awareness of how he is perceived by others. The combination of precise quantitative and qualitative data allows the leader to increase his awareness of where there is a good match and where there are gaps between his current competency performance and what is required for future success.

The quantitative nature of data has a powerful persuasive component from a leader's perspective. Most executives regularly use data to make business decisions. They find the truth that hard numbers bring to be compelling. In this way, data can help the coach expand the leader's awareness of how he is perceived by others. 360-degree feedback (also called multi-rater feedback) is the result of questionnaires completed by the person being coached as well as his boss, peers, direct reports, and other colleagues. The surveys include specific items that address leadership competencies required for the job. I discuss more about how to effectively utilize 360-degree feedback in Chapter 6.

Engaging the Client and "Keeping It Real"

Numbers from questionnaires are not the only data available to the coach. Observation of how the leader is acting during the coaching session itself can also be the basis for powerful feedback. The coaching process is still a human relationship between two people; therefore, a great deal of additional data can also be collected through the actual interaction with the person being coached. You may get information about the leader through personality instruments; however, a good coach learns to develop and rely on her own keen observation skills.

Coaching Tips ...

During each coaching session, ask yourself these questions:

- What am I seeing?
- How am I experiencing this person?
- What am I learning?
- How similar or dissimilar is this person's style to the cultural norm of the organization?
- How different is my experience of this person compared to how he describes himself?

During this step, the coach is putting together a coherent picture of who the leader is, how aware he is of the impact of his behavior, what his personal goals are, and how his goals align with the strategy of the organization. Essentially, the coach and leader work together — using all available feedback and collecting new feedback from others — to create awareness about how the leader is experienced within the context of his job, his coworkers, and his own personal aspirations.

Coaching Tips ...

During subsequent coaching interactions, information is collected directly from the client. This is accomplished by asking good questions, clarifying what is heard, providing feedback, and building on earlier interactions. If you are the coach in this situation, you need to use your personal presence and observation skills. For example, if someone you are coaching seems to come across as being flat, emotionally and verbally, while talking about something critical to his job, you might share this perception with him: "I'm curious about something. You are talking about a very important meeting with your boss, but you seem distant and disinterested. I'm wondering what's going on with you right now?" You could also rephrase the last question: "Are you aware of this contradiction?" Another tactic might be just to ask the client, "What are you aware of right now, as you share this situation with me?" These questions can help the leader get in touch with his feelings; this may be a key component to unlocking a problematic situation.

While the data at the first few meetings might be collected from numerous sources, during subsequent interactions the coach should rely more on his own "in the moment" experience of the leader. The overall goal of this awareness is to understand the impact of the leader's behavior on you, as the coach, which will help you understand his impact on others.

Step Three: Using Action Planning for Competency Development

Once you have collected the additional input, the next step of the coaching process is to jointly review the data with the leader you are coaching. See if the information sheds light on the initial coaching goals and suggests how they may be sharpened or shaped differently. As a manager, you may have worked with a human resources professional or an outside consultant to help you with the 360-degree feedback process. However, it is critical that you take an active role at this step. When I am asked to work with a leader and provide 360-degree feedback, I always strongly encourage the leader to meet with her boss, review the data, and agree on a competency development plan. In some of these situations, the manager then assumes the role of coach and continues to meet with the leader over an extended period of time, using the competency action plan as a reference point in the coaching meetings. Even in instances where I continue to coach the leader, I want the leader's manager to stay active in the process as well. This may mean periodically having a three-way meeting that includes the leader being coached, his boss, and the executive coach. These are opportunities to revisit the goals that were set on competency development and to discuss progress made.

Coaching Tips ...

Ask the leader what she learned from the 360-degree feedback. When a leader has just received this feedback, you have a great opportunity to ask reflective questions that can assist the leader in thinking about the feedback at a deeper level. Specific questions you can ask are as follows:

■ Are the results the same as or different from what you expected?
■ Did you learn anything that was a surprise?
■ Why do you think the results came out the way they did?
■ Are there any aspects of the data that leave you puzzled or that you want to follow up on and get additional information?

After receiving feedback, people need to focus on competencies that both build on strengths and address gaps. Most leaders have gotten to where they are because of the unique strengths and capabilities that they have. Addressing just the competency weaknesses or gaps in the 360-degree feedback analyses is ineffective because it does not energize the leader to do the work required for sustained behavioral change. As we all know, just dwelling on our weaknesses is depressing and creates inertia, depleting the energy we need to move forward. To work on the areas that may be holding us back, we need to tie the development needs to the bigger picture of how we see ourselves and what we want to create. Motivation to change comes from linking the competency goals to both professional goals and a deeper sense of personal identity.

A Case in Point ...

Dan is the dynamic CEO of an international financial services firm, and called me in to do executive coaching for him and the members of his team. When I gathered 360-degree feedback, it showed that others saw Dan as bright, dedicated to a fault, a great decision-maker, and an action-oriented individual. These competency strengths were reflected in the fact that he turned the sagging profits of the company's U.S. Operations into one of the most profitable in the world. The data from the 360-degree analysis confirmed that people thought Dan was a powerful, dynamic leader who had led the firm through a difficult time.

However, there was a darker side to his charismatic nature. At times, his drive for results made him appear insensitive and abrasive to others. He cut people off at meetings when he disagreed with them and made quick judgments of others' capabilities. He used strong language that offended some people and didn't hide his feelings for people he didn't like.

Dan was not surprised when he got this negative data. His reaction was "that is just who I am." At this point in his career — just a few years away from retirement —he was not motivated to change.

What was instrumental in moving Dan to action was our discussion about the legacy he would leave behind when he retired. Dan had spent his whole career building the business. The ongoing success of the firm and its employees was important to him. I asked Dan questions that encouraged him to reflect on how his own behavior was modeling a negative example that would be emulated by other leaders in the organization. Once he understood how that would be an enduring part of his legacy, he was motivated to change. However, increasing Dan's self-awareness was only the first step in the competency development process.

Look for Patterns of Interaction that Keep the Leader from Progressing

Old habits and patterns keep us stuck in behavior that may have outlived its usefulness, making developing new leadership competencies more difficult. We often fall into these old patterns without even realizing it, especially when under stress. Undoing old habits and replacing them with new ones is hard work for all of us and especially so for leaders. Strengths that have led us to success are particularly difficult to abandon because they have helped us get to where we are today. However, taken to excess, what was initially a strength can deteriorate into a weakness, particularly when it is at the expense of the development of other competencies. Even successful people get derailed when circumstances change and they are unable to give up the old patterns that had worked so well for them in the past.

For example, Dan sometimes felt overwhelmed by the seemingly unrelenting challenges facing the firm, especially when his direct reports didn't share his sense of urgency. At times like these, he became more demanding, which his staff perceived as reactive and coercive. In his mind, he was the one working 14-hour days to turn the business around. When I first worked with Dan, he was quick to point out that business success was measured not only in financial terms but also in terms of the retention and satisfaction of key customers. He understood intellectually that how managers treated employees was directly related to how customers rated the service they received. He came to understand that his own style set the pace in that regard.

Once Dan was motivated to change, the coaching process helped him to break old patterns that he fell back on under stress and to learn alternative strategies. Dan began to identify those moments when he was feeling his frustration mount and he wanted to make a decision and move on. With some coaching, he learned how to slow down just at the moment where he felt the urge to speed up, and take the time to ask more questions to understand the situation from others' viewpoints. I also coached him on problem-solving techniques to create more of a dialogue in an emotionally charged situation so that the solution was one that was shared rather than made by him unilaterally. As Dan let go of some of his need for control, his direct reports were more forthcoming and took more initiative. As his staff felt more comfortable making decisions without being second-guessed all the time, Dan began to relax and a new positive pattern began to take the place of the old debilitating one.

This type of action planning may take a number of coaching sessions and can take place over several months, depending upon the situation and the client. What should clearly emerge from this step is the leader's clarity and commitment to take action and establish a specific direction. Each subsequent coaching session then focuses on the individual steps that are necessary to accomplish the overall action.

Observing the leader also provides the coach with opportunities to give him more immediate feedback in critical events at work and to help him stay the course.

Work on a Few Critical Things that Can Make a Difference

Action planning loses energy for a leader when it is too complex or it seems like the changes required to be truly effective are overwhelming. Leaders are more motivated to change when they feel that they are already successful and that modifying a few targeted behaviors will truly make a difference. If Dan had a laundry list of things to do, he definitely would have felt that change at his stage of the game was not worth the effort. We had to work with Dan to identify a few competency areas where doing something differently would reap an immediate improvement as well as long-term business results; then he was willing to make the effort to change old habits.

Coaching Tips ...

- Identify immediate next steps in implementing the action plan
- Identify what others will see differently if the action plan is successful
- Ask the leader what will be the benefit of exhibiting the targeted competencies
- Ask the leader how the business goals will be impacted with the development of the targeted competencies

---

Step Four: Providing Ongoing Feedback and the Opportunity to Reflect

Once coaching goals and a competency action plan have been established, the leader must try out his new competencies. Learning any new complex behavior or set of skills is usually a reiterative process, whether it is a toddler learning to walk, a person learning a musical instrument, or a leader learning to become a better CEO. The rule of thumb is practice, practice, and practice. At this stage, ongoing feedback is an essential part of the process. Sometimes all we need is that extra support, "sure you can do it," or assurances that we are on the right track. At other times, advice on course correction can help prevent a costly mistake.

The leader is usually trying out the new behaviors over the course of time, and it is useful to have the coach periodically present new ideas throughout the process. If you are a coaching manager you may have more frequent opportunities to observe the leader in action, and you can provide on-the-spot feedback (both positive and negative). The coaching meetings provide a time for reflection on how things are going when the leader is faced with new challenges, what actions are chosen, why these actions seemed the best choice for the situation, what happened when the leader tried them, what was successful, and what remains to be improved.

Coaching Tips ...

During this ongoing period, the coach is a useful person with whom to reflect on what has been accomplished. You might want to ask the leader questions like:

- What was it like to take the new action or try the new behavior?
- What were the intended consequences of this action?
- What were the actual consequences of this action?
- Are you satisfied with these consequences?
- If not, why not?

Throughout these interactions, you should be mindful that the coaching discussions themselves offer rich opportunities for the leader to try out new behaviors. A specific interaction might just be an exploration of how the leader feels about the options being discussed, or it may be a determination of whether the leader is getting what he needs from the coaching relationship, so you might want to ask these questions:

- When you reflect on the different options we discussed, which ones do you think might help you achieve your objective?
- I'm wondering how you are feeling right now about what we just discussed.

Coaching Engagements and Their Natural Life Cycle

Like all other business engagements, the end of the cycle is a good time for both the coach and the leader to reflect together on progress made toward competency goals that were set during the action-planning phase of the coaching process. This phase should also be one where both the coach and the leader must take a moment, reflect, and ask, "How are we doing?" and "What have we learned?"

The coach must demonstrate the same openness to learning as she would want the leader to demonstrate. The coach and the leader are on a journey together. The coach is not only providing advice but is also serving as a model of good assessment and reflection skills. If the coach solicits feedback from the leader on the effectiveness of the coaching and demonstrates her own openness to feedback, this can demonstrate the benefits of a collaborative working relationship. The coach must ask explicitly for feedback: What worked and what didn't? She should also be willing to reflect on her own experience in relation to coaching the leader.

For some leaders, the coaching relationship is the only place they can allow themselves to be vulnerable at work (and possibly in their lives). The reflection step can be a very poignant experience of how these discussions can deepen both the relationship and the learning.

Step Five: Creating an Ongoing Relationship of Support

Unlike therapy, which comes to an official close and terminates the relationship between therapist and patient, coaching offers the opportunity to continue the relationship on a more informal basis over time. Many coaching relationships evolve into a relationship of mutually beneficial support of colleagues. If you are a coaching manager, your coaching relationship will likely continue to some extent as long as this person reports to you. Some managers continue to coach and mentor long after their formal organizational ties are severed. This can be a rich relationship for both parties, evolving over time to be one of close friendship.

For external executive coaches, the engagement period tends to be more formal and time-limited. I like to contract with clients for ongoing coaching that can last a few months to a year, with the opportunity to renew the contract. However, making yourself available to stay in touch, with periodic phone calls or occasional lunches, can offer the psychological rewards of a deeper relationship and the knowledge that you have contributed to someone else's personal growth and success.

If you are a leader, keeping in touch with your coach can provide you with someone who knows you well and can offer an outside perspective in difficult situations. When you are at a turning point in your career, your coach may be an objective third party who can evaluate competing opportunities.

Coaching is an ongoing process. Each coaching session has its own internal rhythm as does the process that occurs over time. Coaching for competencies requires you to do the work that each stage of the relationship requires. Keep in mind that effective coaching is both an art and a science.

References

1. O'Neill, M.B., *Executive Coaching with Backbone and Heart,* Jossey-Bass, San Francisco, CA, 2000.
2. Goleman, D., Boyatzis, R., and McKee, A., *Primal Leadership: Realizing the Power of Emotional Intelligence,* Harvard Business School Press, 2002.

THE COMPETENCIES OF LEADERSHIP

Chapter 4

What Success Looks Like

Part of your job as a leader is to ensure that your team is functioning well and that it contributes to the overall well-being of the company. In my 25 years of experience in this area, I have found that the best way to do that is to evaluate each individual on the team, determine his or her strengths or weaknesses, and then — through coaching — help that team member use those strengths and eliminate (or at least minimize) the weaknesses.

To be effective, the coaching process needs to be built on a solid foundation. Whether the coaching process is directed toward enhancing performance or toward career development, both the coach and the leader must have a clear sense of what success looks like within the organization. It is essential to know what personal characteristics, motives, behaviors, skill, or knowledge — in other words, what competencies — are required of successful leaders.

These competencies may differ from one organization to another and from one position to another within the same company, but experience has shown that certain competencies come up repeatedly across the board — competencies that seem to define leadership potential. In this chapter, we describe 13 of these commonly identified competencies and then describe the coaching strategies that you might use to reinforce these competencies.

Are these tasks — recognizing competencies and coaching your people toward them — your responsibility? Yes and no. In reality, most managers don't have the time or the necessary training. You may bring in someone from HR to implement these programs or hire an outside consultant, but to ensure that such a program is effective, it's essential that you understand the process and its applications to your team, your company, and your bottom line.

The first thing that you must understand is how we define and recognize a leader.

Planting the Seeds of Leadership

What does it take to be a leader? From Alexander the Great to Nelson Mandela, from Gandhi to Golda Meir, leader after leader has emerged through history, each facing a different challenge and each manifesting a wide range of leadership styles and behaviors. However, if you conducted an in-depth analysis of each of the characteristics that enabled each these people to become leaders, you would find that they have many attributes in common (like courage, vision, innovation, etc.). In business terms, we would call these common attributes *core competencies.*

The corporate and nonprofit organizations in which most of us work have recognizable similarities. While the specific competencies required of leaders may differ from one organization to another, some core competencies occur so frequently that they serve as a foundation for the requirements that all leaders need to develop to become effective.

I believe that every leader must possess four foundational requirements; I call them the "SEEDs of leadership." They are as follows:

- **S**ense of purpose
- **E**nergy and optimism
- **E**ngaging the hearts and minds of others
- **D**ecision-making

Seed One: Sense of Purpose

Successful leaders want to make a mark on the world; they want to be known as people who make a difference. While different leaders define this for themselves, they all love what they do and believe wholeheartedly in their businesses' goals and missions. They are passionate about whatever business they are in. Whether it is Mel Ming (the CFO at Sesame Workshop), who is in the business of producing children's educational media and programming around the globe, or

Tom Downs (executive vice president of operations and services at QVC), who has pioneered the changing the face of retailing in America, leaders who are most successful feel that they are on an important mission that makes a contribution to the world. In other words, while effective leaders are vigilant about the economic drivers of their organization, they have to be in the business for a greater purpose than making money. The purpose has to be strong enough to motivate them to make the kinds of commitments and sacrifices that most leaders are known to make.

The ability to be persuasive and move others to action can come from a variety of other sources, such as enthusiasm for outdoing a competitor, engendering respect or fear in others, or outrage at a sense of injustice. However, only a leader's deeper sense of purpose, communicated in a compelling manner, has the potential to enable others to aspire to a worthy cause that is greater than themselves.

It may be easier to be drawn to a sense of purpose in businesses and organizations that have a natural humanistic mission, such as those associated with healthcare or education. However, leaders in industries that are more utilitarian have also been known to draw on a wellspring of leadership that comes from their fundamental love of the business and a desire to be the best.

A Case in Point ...

InterMetro has been in business for nearly 75 years making storage and handling products, such as industrial wire shelving in Wilkes-Barre, PA and four other locations. This is not a business that immediately suggests the passion that comes from a sense of purpose. However, John Nackley, president and CEO, grew up in Wilkes-Barre; he was captain of his high school baseball team. After two successful career opportunities in marketing and sales, he began working at Metro in 1985 and rose through the ranks to become CEO at a time that the business was being challenged by imports. The patent for Metro's key product, which had made the company an industry leader with high market share, had expired, and foreign competition was attempting to garner market share through predatory pricing tactics. Metro held firm longer than most, manufacturing its products in the United States, while new capacity was built in Mexico and sourcing agreements were developed in Asia.

Internally, the company was also in major transition. Although it was privately held for much of its history, the founding ownership eventually sold the company to Bessemer Holdings and subsequently to Fortune 500 giant Emerson, who asked Nackley to stay on as CEO. Facing these challenges, John spoke to us about the pressure for showing short-term profits while investing and building for the future.

John Nackley feels he has to fight to assure the long-term competitiveness of InterMetro globally in concert with securing the future of the company and its place in Wilkes-Barre. This clear and overriding sense of purpose has motivated him to remain committed to the job. As he put it, "There is an underlying commitment that keeps me here today. It is my commitment to our people, the industry, our customers, and our presence in the community. I am committed to delivering results to Emerson, because that is who ultimately pays me, and I support their business philosophy and process — but the first and foremost reason that I stay connected is because of this commitment to the people I work with, and to the heritage of Metro and what it stands for."

Coaching Tips ...

- **Find out what makes the leader feel motivated and energized** — You can't give a leader a sense of purpose. Many leaders, like John Nackley, are already quite eloquent on what excites them and keeps them dedicated. Others have not yet stopped to think about the question. In these cases, you can help the leader to clarify his personal values. Discuss his personal background, and discover what past accomplishments he is proudest of. This can help identify and clarify a personal sense of mission and passion.

- **Help the leader become more aware of what values are most important to her and how these values connect to the company's values and mission —**

Leaders' commitment can be applied to any of the stakeholders in a company. Customers want quality products and services delivered on time at a fair price. Shareholders want profits, dividends, and financial rewards. Employees want fair compensation, job security, a decent working environment, challenging work, and future opportunity. Any of these can be an avenue that creates meaning and purpose for the leader, but the key is that it has to be something the leader feels passionate about. In the 1996 article "Destiny and the job of the leader," published in *Fast Company* magazine, Joe Jaworski, formally with Royal/Shell's scenario planning group, put it this way: "Before you can lead others, before you can help others, you have to discover yourself .... If you want a creative explosion to take place, if you want the kind of performance that leads to truly exceptional results, you have to be willing to embark on a journey that leads to an alignment between an individual's personal values and aspirations and the values and aspirations of the company."

You can empower people to create a future that they truly desire by getting them to discover what they passionately care about.

Seed Two: Energy and Optimism

All successful leaders have a tremendous sense of self-confidence that is characterized by energy and optimism. They developed a can-do attitude early in life. A sense of possibilities allowed them to take risks, learn from experience, and ultimately succeed in a broader playing field than the world in which they grew up. Self-confident leaders also tend to be results-oriented people who stay focused on the satisfaction achieved in reaching a goal. They are less likely to become derailed by setbacks; they see the setbacks instead as opportunities to learn and improve their strategies. Achieving goals builds self-confidence, so this optimistic attitude becomes self-reinforcing.

Self-confident leaders are more likely to take risks and do things for the good of the business, regardless of whether these things are initially popular. They are more likely to speak up in difficult situations or coach a subordinate who is having difficulties. Optimistic leaders are also more likely to see the positive qualities in others. Where pessimists frequently zero in others' faults and shortcomings, optimists can see the strengths and potential of those they lead. A good deal of research has been done over the years on the Pygmalion Effect and the power of positive expectations, the concept that was made famous in the movie *My Fair Lady*. When Eliza Doolittle is transformed from a flower girl into a believable aristocrat through the (albeit imperfect) coaching of her tutor, Henry Higgins. The Pygmalion effect, simply stated, is that when you expect the best in people, you help them expect the best from themselves. This positive optimism can be contagious. Leaders who feel positive about themselves are more likely to invest their energy in developing those who work for them and to infuse a dynamic of positive energy into their organization's culture.

A Case in Point …

Mel Ming, currently the chief financial officer at Children's Television Network, told us a story of one of the tougher but ultimately rewarding dilemmas he faced earlier in his career, when he was a senior manager at Coopers & Lybrand. One of his indirect reports, Igor, had great technical skills and was ambitious and bright. But Igor was not able to build relationships with his colleagues, who perceived him as stubborn, arrogant, and a loner.

When a supervisory position became available, Igor applied for it, but no one supported him but Mel. Mel saw Igor as someone with tremendous drive, commitment, and intelligence — who needed to be coached. He was able to see Igor's strengths, not just his shortcomings. Mel promoted him to supervisor — on the condition that Igor meet with him on a regular basis over the course of the next two years. Mel's belief in Igor, demonstrated in his coaching sessions, was just what Igor needed to bolster his self-confidence and to make him an effective leader.

Coaching Tips ...

Work with leaders to expand their understanding of the different realms and constituencies they need to effectively manage and impact. Most people who lack confidence derail before they assume a leadership position. In this sense, self-confidence is very much a price of admission to the leadership ranks. However, self-confidence is rarely an all-or-nothing thing. Some leaders are confident in some areas, perhaps in decision-making and marketing, but less confident in others, such as building an organizational culture where people feel valued. Like all of us, leaders prefer to spend their time in the areas in which they feel successful, and they tend to devote less attention to areas where they feel uncertain. As a coach, your job is to expand the leader's awareness of the importance of the areas that require more of his attention. Part of effective coaching is helping a leader to have a greater sense of self-awareness as well as to have the necessary skills to handle difficult situations in which the leader is less comfortable.

Seed Three: Engaging the Hearts and Minds of Others

Leaders who get exceptional results inspire others to give the discretionary effort that goes beyond the fundamentals of doing a good job. They are effective at building relationships and emotionally connecting with others around the vision and the mission of the business. They are generous in sharing the recognition and publicly crediting others for the organization's successes. Conversely, when problems occur, these leaders first look at their own accountability and have the courage to admit their own mistakes rather than to blame others.

A Case in Point ...

Tom Kaney of Glaxo/SmithKline tells the story of a scientist of world-class brilliance, a man he describes as having an infinite knowledge about every aspect of the current and future state of biological sciences — but who had no concept of the necessity of "playing well with others." The scientist believed that staying on the cutting edge of his discipline would get him and his organization the recognition he wanted. Unfortunately, he was never able to fulfill his potential as a company leader. More than that, he proved to be an impediment to others in making the scientific progress that is so essential for a pharmaceutical company like Glaxo/SmithKline. Here's how Tom described his executive colleague: "He was a brilliant intellectual and rational thinker. But he just couldn't sense or see the emotional side of the organization — how to enroll people, how to empower people, how to get behind them. All he could see was the importance of being the smartest guy on top of the pyramid. He constantly took the wind out of people's intellectual and emotional sails. Without ever intending to do so, he created an atmosphere of fear and caution in the pursuit of business results, rather than one of risk-taking and innovation. His great strength became a radical weakness. It was a blind spot that was never dealt with."

It would be difficult, if not impossible, for that executive to engage the hearts and minds of others. His peers and colleagues, well aware of his overriding self-interest, could never trust him. Where there is trust between a leader and those around him, there is also the potential for influence — the ability to engage the hearts of people as well as their heads. This involves the delicate understanding and sensitive handling of other people's emotions — emotions that are contagious, particularly in times of dynamic change or organizational stress.

Emotions are contagious. In his book *Emotional Intelligence,* Daniel Goleman explains, "in subtle (or not so subtle) ways, we all make each other feel a bit better (or a lot worse)." It's a simple concept that applies to the workplace and every other place. We all affect each other's emotions. If one person feels good about what he's doing, or feels like he's making an important contribution to his team, it makes everyone on the team feel good — and encourages them to contribute that extra effort that can make a great difference to the organization as a whole. As a leader, you have an opportunity to make a substantial impact on your organization — either positive or negative. For example, in most organizations, everyone focuses quickly on a rapid decline in sales or a coming wave of layoffs. But a leader who is skilled in impact and influence is more likely to manage or steer these emotional currents rather than to be pulled under by them. In other words, your ability to remain optimistic, positive, and enthusiastic can influence others to develop the same core competencies.

Coaching Tips ...

Get to know the leader you are coaching and help her to use her strengths to better advantage. Fortunately, many leadership styles can be effective in engaging others and leading them to action. Some leaders are highly charismatic, lively public speakers who exude confidence, while others are just as effective with a sincere but much lower-key, humble approach. Like the other competencies I have been discussing, the first step is to provide the leader with sufficient feedback so that she understands the perceptions of others and sees how they stack up to her own self-perceptions.

Engaging the hearts and minds of others leads to building a climate of trust and employee commitment. Later in this chapter, we detail some of the competencies that are frequently used by leaders to engage others and to create a sense of trust and loyalty with those who work in their organization.

Seed Four: Decision-Making

While emotional competencies have recently received a lot of attention in the business press, the thinking competencies have been pushed to the background. Yet it is clear that outstanding leaders require proficiency in cognitive competencies as well as emotional competencies. Knowledge of your specific industry, the ability to see trends and the implications for your business, and a keen intellect are always in high demand. While a variety of competencies are important in this area (which I discuss later in this chapter), the capacity to make good decisions stands out as one of the most significant requirements of effective leadership. The ability to make decisions that others view as timely, wise, ethical, and in the business's best interest contributes to the leader's power base. Leaders are willing to make the tough decisions and take risks, and they "know when to hold them and when to fold them."

Good decision-making is a complex skill. First, the effectiveness of good decisions lies less in the answers the decisions provide than in the quality of the questions asked. It is the ability to seek relevant information that directly contributes to quality decisions. Arrogant leaders may prematurely make decisions without enough input from people who are directly involved with the problem at hand. An effective decision-maker is usually a good listener and is open to learning from others. Always on the lookout for meaningful data, this leader is thirsty for information, whether it's analyzing the performance numbers of the company or listening to customers and employees.

A Case in Point ...

Tom Downs is executive vice president of operations at QVC, the original home shopping channel that has expanded worldwide. Seven thousand people directly or indirectly report to him. This is a lot of people to stay in touch with, and there are many levels of supervisors between Tom, the customer service operators, and the people who ship the goods from warehouses scattered throughout the company and abroad. Tom often felt like he was making decisions for these people without knowing exactly how the decisions would affect them. He needed to find a way to be more in touch with his employees.

Like many companies, QVC's headquarters is a smoke-free environment. However, there is an outdoor gazebo where smokers can take a break. Even though Tom doesn't smoke, he frequently visits the smoking gazebo. He says it is one place where he can really hear what is going on throughout the company. As Tom said when I interviewed him, "That's the place I go when I want to know what people really think. When I come back inside, I smell like an old stinky cigarette — but I come in with a lot of information I wouldn't otherwise have. It's my way of keeping in touch with my hourly employees. They may be nervous when they first see me coming out there, but then they start talking, and before I know it, they're unloading all of their issues and concerns. I learn more out there then I do sitting in my office, and it gives me the information I need to make the best decisions."

A second component of effective decision-making is knowing who should be involved in the decision-making process. We are long past the days of autocratic leaders who always made decisions on their own. Empowerment and employee involvement, buzzwords of the 1980s and 1990s, require that authority and accountability — and hence decision-making — be distributed throughout an organization. While many issues are best handled by involving a broader group, a leader still needs to keep certain decisions close to the vest. Sorting out who should be involved in which kinds of issues is often an underpinning of effective leadership.

A Case in Point …

One fast-growing entrepreneurial company I worked with had a CEO who recruited two seasoned executives in marketing and sales, both with years of experience working for larger competitors. However, once these executives were on board, the CEO had difficulty letting go of some of the decisions that for years had fallen under his domain. As his coach, I initiated several discussions of his role and his executives' roles, and suggested how he could set up new mechanisms for decision-making.

This company had recently acquired several new businesses, and the sales territories needed to be reorganized to increase efficiency and to decrease duplication of effort. Since the CEO had been with the company for 25 years, he was reluctant to delegate the decision for such an important priority. The company had no processes or procedures, such as routine executive committee meetings, for making decisions like this. Part of my coaching effort was setting up these processes, which ultimately meant getting the CEO to delegate this planning to the two executives who were directly accountable for the results of the sales efforts.

Coaching Tips ...

Help your leaders sort out which kinds of decisions to make alone, which kinds to make with the input from others, which kinds to make through consensus of the entire executive team, and which kinds to delegate to others.

An Overview of Competencies for Leadership

These four "SEEDs" are the entry requirements of effective leadership. Without at least some ability in each of these four areas, it is unlikely that an individual will be an effective leader.

However, many other competencies are also important, some of which can be readily developed on the job. It would be impossible to include here all the variations of leadership competencies that exist. Instead, I will provide you with examples of the kinds of competencies that most frequently appear as part of a leadership model. This overview is organized into four specific groups that I call *competency clusters* (see Figure 4.1). They are as follows:

- Personal effectiveness
- Managing others
- Communication
- Thinking

I also provide a few suggestions for the development of each competency that I have found to be useful in my own coaching practice. More exhaustive published compendiums of development suggestions are available; two good publications that every coach should have on his shelf are *The Successful Manager's Handbook,* published by Personnel Decisions International, and *The Career Architect Development Planner,* written by Michael M. Lombardo and Robert W. Eichinger and published by Lominger Limited.

Competencies for Leadership

Personal Effectiveness	Communication
Self Awareness Courage Achieving Results through Others Self-Control	Interpersonal Sensitivity Impact and Influence Political Awareness
Managing Others	Thinking
Providing Direction Developing Organizational Talent Teamwork	Strategic Thinking Integrity

Figure 4.1 Competencies for leadership.

Personal Effectiveness Cluster

These competencies determine how we manage ourselves and draw on inner strengths. They are typically the competencies that a leader has drawn on since childhood, and they have been instrumental in creating the self-motivation required to achieve a leadership position. Competencies frequently found in this domain are as follows:

- Self-awareness
- Courage
- Achieving results through others
- Initiative
- Self-control

The Competency of Self-Awareness

Self-awareness is the ability to be aware of, recognize, and understand one's strengths and weaknesses as well as one's emotional responses to a situation. It is important for leaders to have a reasonable idea of how they see themselves, how they are perceived by the people they work with, and how they influence what happens around them or because of them. Leaders who, like ostriches, would prefer to have their head in the sand are also likely to be closed-minded when it comes to new ideas. This is short-sighted, particularly when competitors are likely to be closely watching a leader's performance, hoping to take advantage of his or her vulnerabilities.

Coaching Strategies — Self-Awareness

- **A map is not the territory** — The overall feedback strategies that form the basis of this book can provide the map to the road to self-awareness. However, a map, no matter how good, is just a tool. Sometimes leaders who are successful become blinded by their own success; they either don't seek feedback or don't take anything they perceive as criticism seriously. If you are a coach, the way to address this is to link the feedback to a business consequence that is important to the leader.
- **Learn from experience** — One of the differentiating characteristics of successful people is their ability to learn and grow as a result of both their successes and mistakes. Leaders need to be aware of how they are impacting others and to know how that is impacting the results they are achieving. It a good idea to debrief critical meetings, sales calls, or project reviews with a trusted colleague or a coach by asking the following questions:
  - What did we learn?
  - What should we do differently next time?
  - How else could we have prepared for the situation?
  - Did we judge others' motives correctly in the situation?

The Competency of Courage

Courage is a competency that is closely related to self-awareness. It takes a high level of bravery to honestly appraise your own strengths and weaknesses. But the courage required for leaders goes beyond self-knowledge; it also requires taking an honest appraisal of the business situation and being able to make the tough decisions, regardless of whether they are popular at the time. Courage involves acting on the strength of your own convictions.

Coaching Strategies — Courage

- **Say what needs to be said** — Courage in the workplace often involves a leader saying what needs to be said, even when it is difficult. As a coach, you can demonstrate this by bringing up difficult issues in a direct but diplomatic fashion. If you have to deliver negative feedback, be succinct and don't waste time on a long preamble. Demonstrate that saying difficult things means being honest and taking a risk, but being compassionate in the process.

■ **Be brave, be bold** — If you are working with a leader who needs to take a risk, get her to imagine what success might look like. When people can imagine a successful outcome, they are more apt to try new things to get better results. Remind the leader that making mistakes is a natural consequence of trying new behaviors or doing something unfamiliar. Start in a safe environment, where the ramifications of making mistakes are not severe and where you can view failure as a part of the learning process.

The Competency of Achieving Results through Others

Achieving results through others is often the cornerstone of a leader's success. Most executives have a strong track record: they've either produced impressive bottom-line results or they have made a strong contribution in a specialty area. Their drive for achievement helped them reach their current level of success. But the drive for achievement is a mixed blessing. Because once at the top, requirements change, and a leader must now create newer and broader vistas for achievement, many of which can only be accomplished by incorporating other people into the leader's mission. Achievement is no longer a personal or parochial matter. At the higher levels, leaders must learn to transmit their leadership throughout the organization, and they can't do that single-handedly. At a certain point, what's required is less, not more, reliance on personal, individual effort in functional areas. Effective leadership requires giving up the satisfaction and recognition that are intrinsic to personal accomplishment and placing greater trust and confidence in the collective efforts of others.

Coaching Strategies — Achieving Results through Others

■ **Management 101** — Because most people in a leadership role have already demonstrated a track record of achieving results, the role of the coach is to assist these people in shifting gears and understanding the additional competencies that are required to inspire others to the same level of performance. This usually requires diagnosing what is missing in the leader's management skills. Some leaders need to learn to delegate more and to stop micromanaging, while other leaders don't realize that they are not clearly communicating goals or setting realistic performance standards.

▪ **Work on the few things that can make a difference** — If a leader is not getting the results the organization expects, the coach and the leader need to take a good look at the obstacles that are impeding the expected progress. Be realistic about the things that are at least partially under the leader's control (competencies such as relationships with others, judgment of the situation, planning and organizing, etc.) and the things that are outside of the leader's control (usually environmental or organizational factors such as market conditions, changing managerial structure, or access to resources). Work with the leader to prioritize the few things over which he has control and where developing competencies can have a big impact on his goals. As a coach, you can acknowledge the leader's frustrations without necessarily concluding that others are to blame and without vindicating the leader from taking accountability.

The Competency of Initiative

Initiative is frequently a key competency in leadership because it characterizes people who seize opportunities and are ready to act. Like achievement motivation, this competency is learned and reinforced early in life. Propelled by the seed of optimism and energy, leaders with initiative are more likely to bounce back from setbacks or failures. They go the extra mile and give the discretionary effort rather than seeing extra work as being "not my job." Individuals with this competence also cut through red tape and bend the rules when necessary. Their own enterprising efforts can be a catalyst to mobilize others into action.

Coaching Strategies — Initiative

▪ **Identify what being proactive would look like in your organization** — Successful leaders don't wait to be asked but are the ones to seize opportunities, make suggestions, and sell their ideas. Taking the initiative requires both a degree of risk-taking and salesmanship. It is not uncommon for organizations to reject unsolicited new ideas, even if they are offered from someone who is at the top of the organization. However, as a coach you should be letting the leader know that just because there is initial resistance, this doesn't mean that the ideas are not worthwhile or that people won't ultimately accept them. In other words, it is worth taking a risk. Perseverance is a key factor in the initiative competency. Discuss why the leader has been reluctant to demonstrate initiative in the past. Together identify some opportunities for the leader to start demonstrating this competency, and coach her through the steps that would likely create some early successes.

- **Promote your ideas** — It is not uncommon that development in initiative simultaneously requires development of impact and influence skills. It is one thing to offer new ideas, and it is another to gain the political support from others. Look at what the feedback suggests on the relationship of these two competencies for each leader you are working with.

The Competency of Self-Control

Self-control is the ability to keep one's emotional reactions to situations in check. It also includes thinking clearly under pressure. No leader can afford to be controlled by feelings of frustration, disappointment, or anger. Leading people can be anxiety-provoking. Leaders who don't exercise self-control and vent their feelings in front of others often provoke negative responses from others. Learning to manage your moods and to understand how they impact your decision-making is ultimately one of the more profound personal responsibilities of a leader.

Coaching Strategies — Self-Control

- **Understand emotional triggers** — Self-awareness is the first step for a leader to understand his own emotional patterns and to see how his feelings can create a knee-jerk reaction to situations. When people become emotional, they are less likely to think clearly. Stressful situations often trigger negative emotions of fear, anger, frustration, anxiety, or defeat, and these feelings can color our judgments and reactions to others. Under stress, we can mistakenly personalize situations and react defensively. Discuss with the leader specific occasions where he showed a lack of self-control, and see if the two of you can identify the pattern of what triggered the response. Develop some achievable goals to gradually decrease the frequency of outbursts, control impulsiveness, and increase abilities to manage stress and calm others.

■ **Express how you feel without venting emotion** — As a coach, you can work with the leader you are coaching to resist the temptation to display strong emotion. It takes practice to continue to talk and act calmly in stressful situations. Avoiding situations that create these negative feelings is unrealistic, and bottling up negative feelings is unhealthy. However, a leader can be more effective if he expresses his feelings verbally without fully demonstrating them. For example, if an important deadline is missed, it is appropriate for the leader to say he is frustrated and disappointed without adding the emotional display. By contrast, an emotional display of anger or rage only triggers a "fight or flight" reaction in the other person and can paralyze the two people from rectifying the situation.

Managing Others Cluster

These are the competencies that include the abilities leaders demonstrate in getting work done through others. They frequently include the competencies of:

- Providing direction
- Developing organizational talent
- Teamwork

The Competency of Providing Direction

Providing direction is the competency that includes the skills, behaviors, and abilities that are required to provide focus and direction for work activities. People are the most productive when they have a clear sense of what is important and what is expected of them. Providing direction often includes telling people what to do, setting expectations and limits, and confronting performance problems directly.

The hallmark of an effective leader is the ability to generate a vision and then establish goals and priorities that are aligned with the vision. Once that vision is clarified, a leader must set priorities as well as clarify roles and responsibilities. Knowing others' strengths and weaknesses gives the leader the opportunity to make things happen through others by giving direct reports the authority and autonomy to make decisions that are appropriate to their level of responsibility and competency in the job.

Coaching Strategies — Providing Direction

- **Communicate objectives** — Encourage the leader to present her personal objectives to her direct reports in a clear and direct manner (for example, at a major meeting at the beginning of the year). She should be clear about how the overall organizational objectives are linked to her personal objectives and how these are, in turn, accomplished through her direct reports' individual efforts. You can be a sounding board to make sure that the leader is clear about her expectations of each of her direct reports. Together, document a performance plan for the year.
- **Assist the leader in getting into the habit of thinking ahead** — Ensure that the leader has a system in place to review the status of current projects and to identify any issues of concern before they become obstacles to a project's success. The leader should be periodically checking in with employees over the course of a project to see how they are proceeding.
- **Clarify roles and responsibilities** — When people aren't sure who is supposed to do what and when the lines of accountability are vague, the implementation of large-scale efforts can falter. Work with the leader to clarify and communicate her goals. Then help her plan to get the team together to discuss how they will achieve those goals and to clarify and negotiate their individual roles.

The Competency of Developing Organizational Talent

This competency takes a genuine commitment to foster long-term growth and development of employees, in order to use their talents for current and future needs of the business. This competency includes the skills to coach others, set goals, monitor others' performance, and give timely feedback. One of the seeds of this competency is the desire to "engage the hearts and minds of others." Leaders who excel at this competency are able to gain others' commitment because they have devoted their time and attention to helping these people succeed. These leaders also contribute to the organization's success by growing talent within the company.

Leaders need to be concerned with not only their direct reports but also in ensuring that the organization is a learning community where everyone must be prepared to coach and learn from anyone. "It all comes back to competencies," says Catharine Newberry, vice president at Aventis-Pasteur. "If you're hiring the right people and holding them accountable for performance, if you're doing a better job of making selections based on competencies, then you can afford to trust the people who are in those roles — because you've already asked a lot of really important questions about the set of behaviors a person is likely to present in certain circumstances. You know from the data that this person's judgment is trustworthy. Then you put the person in the job and say, 'Here's your mission; go for it,' and you trust them to do it."

Coaching Strategies — Developing Organizational Talent

- **Develop an organizational coaching plan** — The coaching process often helps kick-start an enhanced focus of development for employees at all levels. Once the leader has experienced the value of receiving feedback, she has personal experience on how important individual development is to organizational success.
- **Succession planning for development** — Review the leader's succession plan, and determine what he is doing to develop his leaders for the future. Ensure that the leader is seeking developmental opportunities for his people that will stretch their capabilities with future organizational needs in mind.

The Competency of Teamwork

Teamwork is a competency that is important to executives, both as leaders and as team members. Leaders who are effective in this competency understand the importance of collaboration and are themselves models of respect, helpfulness, and collegiality. Their own behavior sets a positive tone for the team, and others are drawn into the supportive environment. These leaders know how to balance the need to get the job done with paying attention to others' emotional needs. They cultivate strong social bonds to be channeled into achievement for the team. Leaders who are effective at teamwork value diversity in the group and model openness to others who are different than they are. They ensure that everyone shares the credit and recognition for accomplishments. A 1996 study by the Center for Creative Leadership pointed out that the top reason that senior executives derail in their careers is that they are unable to manage a team.

Coaching Strategies — Teamwork

- **Leaders need to build team spirit** — Work with the leader to enhance the team dynamic of his direct reports or other teams he manages. How does he use staff meetings? With what frequency do they occur? Are they used primarily for information sharing, or is time allotted for joint problem-solving? Do the team members know each other on a personal basis? What is the level of trust among the team members? Do team members understand how their individual success is interdependent on each other's success?
- **Every team leader is also a team member** — Is the leader you are coaching viewed as a valued collaborator among his peers? If you have 360-degree feedback, ratings by peers are often a good indicator of teamwork. If the leader has a deficiency in this area, work with her to build the relationships that are required to establish trust.

Communication Cluster

This is the group of competencies that focus on the leader's ability to communicate with and persuade others and to create allies for his stated organizational purpose, mission, values, and strategy. These competencies are rooted in the third seed of leadership — engaging the hearts and minds of others, which I discussed earlier in this chapter. The specific competencies that are typically included in this cluster include:

- Interpersonal sensitivity
- Impact and influence
- Political awareness

The Competency of Interpersonal Sensitivity

Interpersonal sensitivity is the ability to listen with empathy and to read the feelings of others from their nonverbal cues, along with the desire to understand others. It takes courage to genuinely appreciate where someone else is coming from, particularly if you don't agree with her position. It requires restraint, respect, and even the ability to share control with the other person. As John Nackley of InterMetro told me in his interview, "Interpersonal skills are the number one skill required by successful executives. It's difficult to provide leadership without these critical skills."

Coaching Strategies — Interpersonal Sensitivity

- **Model the behavior** — As a coach, you have a powerful opportunity to model the interpersonal sensitivity that you want to see in the leader. Asking reflective questions ("How did you feel when he didn't mention your name during the presentation?") and paraphrasing ("What I hear you saying is, when Joe doesn't answer your e-mails, you become really annoyed.") are two techniques that most leaders can easily learn through coaching. You can show the leader how to use these skills to more easily connect with other people's feelings and thoughts. In the coaching session, point out when you are using these techniques and then ask the leader to try them out with you. If the leader can get comfortable using these techniques with his coach, he is more likely to try them when difficult situations occur in everyday life.
- **Stop avoiding difficult people** — We all have more trouble with some people than with others, and the easy, and ineffective, solution is to avoid contact. Leaders can't have that luxury. Encourage the leader you are coaching to reflect on why he doesn't like someone and how avoiding him or her is impacting the business. To help the leader work more effectively with difficult people, help him see the situation from their perspectives. To improve a relationship, you have to work at it and through coaching, plan a strategy to establish a degree of reciprocity.

The Competency of Impact and Influence

This competency is the ability to convince other people of your point of view and win support for your ideas. There is nothing so beneficial to the organization as a leader's ability to "make something happen." People who are adept at influence are able to move everyone forward to supporting the same goal, even if it is not immediately apparent how the goal will serve everyone's self-interest. These leaders are typically effective at things such as negotiating persuasively, getting others to take action, and commanding the attention and respect of others.

Leaders with impact and influence often take dramatic action to make a point. They are also adept at building support for ideas behind the scenes. Looking to the future, it appears that leaders in the business, government, and nonprofit world will need increasingly sophisticated skills in this competence.

Coaching Strategies — Impact and Influence

- **Tailor your influence strategy** — In the coaching session, help the leader think through how she is going to sell an important, but perhaps unpopular, idea. Who are the important stakeholders? Does she have positive relationships in place with critical people or "opinion leaders" who can provide influence behind the scenes on her behalf? Has she analyzed her audience and tailored her presentation to fit their interests and attention spans? Has she anticipated objections and how she will counter them? Bringing up these topics in a coaching session can assist the leader in thinking through all the aspects of a situation that calls for impact and influence.

- **Observe the leader in action** — Effective influence is not just the result of careful preparation but also represent the leader's ability to establish rapport in the moment. If you observe the leader in action, you can see if she has any blind spots that may be limiting her ability to win support for her ideas. Some of these blind spots may include taking too strong a stand for a narrow issue, not being politically savvy, or not reading others' nonverbal cues.

The Competency of Political Awareness

Political awareness is a competency that is critical for balancing the conflicting interests and viewpoints inside and outside of the organization. People without political awareness are oblivious to the informal relationships around them and how these relationships impact decision-making. Many high achievers tend to feel that if you just work hard and do the right things, good efforts will speak for themselves. Because these achievers underestimate the impact that others can have on gaining support for ideas and proposals, they are often blindsided and caught by surprise when things don't go their way. They frequently dissociate their own behavior from its consequences. And, in so doing, these achievers unwittingly sabotage their own agenda for getting things done.

Coaching Strategies — Political Awareness

■ **Organizations are political arenas where people have big egos and strong ambitions** — To be successful, a leader cannot disdain organizational politics but must learn how to think about power relationships and the impact they have on getting things done in a large organization. As a coach, you need to understand the organizational culture in which the leader works so you can understand his power position relative to others in the organization. Understanding the organizational politics can help the leader avoid either stepping on other people's toes or getting blindsided.

■ **Work your network for competitive advantage** — Senior leaders sometimes forget how important it is to continue to build relationships with a broad cross section of people, including one's supervisor, customers, colleagues, and vendors as well as the larger business community. Having a broad network of people as allies helps build a foundation for ideas and programs that the leader wants to sponsor or implement. Help the leader analyze his current network and determine where significant gaps exist. Take the time to develop a game plan to expand the leader's network as well as to maintain regular contact with those who are key opinion leaders.

Thinking Cluster

While these competencies are not as clearly joined to the emotional intelligence paradigm as the others we have discussed, they remain a critical part of an effective leader's skills and are grounded in the fourth seed of leadership — decision-making. Included in this group are:

■ Strategic thinking
■ Integrity

The Competency of Strategic Thinking

Strategic thinking is the ability to assess rapidly changing trends, market opportunities, and the competition. It includes the capacity to make an honest assessment of the organization's capabilities to meet these challenges both in terms of strengths and weaknesses. Understanding the business is a critical component of strategic thinking. Analyzing opportunities and problems from a broad perspective, planning solutions, and anticipating the reactions of others are all integral to this competency.

A leader gains credibility by being known as a strategic thinker. To be viewed as an expert resource across the organization, a leader needs to be knowledgeable about future industry trends and competitive forces and must be able to identify key success factors for her own organization. The successful leader can focus the organization's resources and initiatives in areas that have the greatest long-term gain, whether that entails entering new markets, investing in technology, or divesting divisions that are not core to the business mission.

Coaching Strategies — Strategic Thinking

■ **Ensure that strategies of prior success don't lull the leader into complacency** — As we have seen in the spectacular rise and fall of industries that once saw themselves as indomitable, if you don't get ahead of the competition, it will get ahead of you.
■ **Scan the environment** — Assist the leader in developing his abilities and systems to keep abreast of new market developments, track the competition, and develop an in-depth understanding of the business environment. This may involve establishing a system to gather competitive intelligence, emerging ideas and changes in your business.
■ **Schedule a retreat** — Help the leader plan to use the time away from the office to address strategic issues facing her team.

Use this as an opportunity for the team to think about how they can apply a broader perspective to their activities and surface emerging ideas.

The Competency of Integrity

Integrity is the ability to know right from wrong. As the unfortunate proliferation of corporate scandals has shown, all leaders are occasionally placed in compromising situations. The offending companies have shown the country, by negative example, the strength of character that is required to demonstrate integrity when the pressure is on to keep stock prices up or to show other short-term results. Leaders who demonstrate integrity handle sensitive issues fairly and with discretion, and they take actions that don't compromise their values or those of the organization. Integrity is the basis of trust and is the result of a leader whose actions are consistent with her words.

Coaching Strategies — Integrity

- **Recognize when integrity is a personality issue** — If integrity comes out of 360-degree feedback as a development issue, the coach and leader need to look at the data honestly and determine at what level integrity is seen as a problem. If the issue is honesty or a tendency to color the facts to further personal ambitions, coaching may not be sufficient to address the underlying issues; this behavior may be due to powerful personality disorders that are unlikely to fundamentally change the person.
- **Understand that overcommitment can be seen as a breach of integrity** — More frequently, integrity is in question when a leader makes agreements or commitments that others perceive are broken. If a leader is seen as promising one thing and delivering another, this can lower the climate of trust within the team. As a coach, the following points are good reminders for a leader who has a tendency to overcommit:
  - Choose your commitments carefully. Figure out how you will follow through on the agreement before making commitments to others.
  - Resist the tendency to make commitments in order to buy more time or keep others from bothering you.

- Realize that a failure to meet deadlines is sometimes seen as a lack of integrity by others.

It's All about Balance

In the real world, there are many kinds of effective leaders. It's not important that they have one particular competency versus another but that they have the right mix of competencies. It is all about balance. A leader who is stellar in the thinking competencies but has neither an aptitude for nor interest in communicating with or managing others is doomed to fail in a leadership role.

In the next chapter, I will discuss a range of approaches that are effective for identifying the leadership competencies important to your unique business.

References

1. Webber, A.M., Destiny and the job of the leader, *Fast Company,* June 1996, 40.
2. Goleman, D., *Emotional Intelligence,* Bantam Books, New York, 1995.
3. Davis, B.L. (editor), *Successful Manager's Handbook,* Personnel Decisions International, Minneapolis, MN, 1996.
4. Lombardo, M. and Eichinger, R.W., *The Career Architect Development Planner,* Lominger Limited, Minneapolis, MN, 1999.
5. Leslie, J.B. and Van Velsor, E., A look at derailment today: North America and Europe, Center for Creative Leadership, Greensboro, NC, 1996.

Chapter 5

Developing Models for Coaching Success

The last chapter provided you with an overview of certain competencies that show up repeatedly in effective leaders. In this chapter, we talk about how you can identify a set of competencies that accurately predict what outstanding performance would look like in a particular job or role.

Suppose your ultimate goal is to evaluate Bob Smith, who is currently vice president of marketing. You begin by asking yourself, "What am I trying to get the VP of marketing to accomplish? What results are most important to his team and this company?" Then, you would determine what qualities a person would need to attain these results. You could find these qualities by using empirical data from other people who have held this position — and have been outstanding. These data may come from people in your own company, or they may come from a generalized list of competencies that outside research has shown to be effective for people in Bob's position.

When you have listed the qualities that make up your ideal VP of marketing, you have built a competency model: a group of identified competencies that distinguish leadership in a given role or organization.

Recognizing these competencies can tell you whether your people are performing their jobs at the level required to succeed in business today. Because it is possible to both measure and learn the behaviors that these competencies require, they are an ideal set of benchmarks for the coaching process. The result is that people know what is expected of them and are motivated to reach those expectations; this not only improves their individual performance but also matches what the organization needs them to do.

Ellen Petersen, former vice president at Aramark Corporation, says that competencies are "a perfect way to start coaching, to say, 'Let's agree on our starting point. Here are the competencies for the job you've got, and on which you're currently being measured. And here are the competencies you'll need to get to the next level.' When you can get people to agree on these factors right off the bat, your job as a coach is much easier, and their progress and motivation are effectively increased."

The more specifically the leadership requirements can be researched and identified for each organization, the greater the likelihood that coaching will have a greater impact for both the leader being coached and the organization as a whole. Generic, standardized models that are available may be all you need. Then there are more complex programs that require highly trained consultants. Obviously, it would be ideal to have customized competency models designed for your unique company. But a few critical business decisions can help you determine whether to make this investment and just how specifically designed your competency models should be, including time frames and budgets, and whether the positions being evaluated have a direct impact on your bottom line.

At the organizational level, competency models are powerful because they help align behavior from one individual to another. By using competencies to guide behavior, the leadership team can strive for a consistency among themselves that recognizes and rewards the same attributes. For example, had integrity been a defined and rewarded competency in many of today's embattled corporations, perhaps these companies would not find themselves in their current difficulties.

Competencies work best when they become deeply ingrained in both the values of the organization and in the performance that is expected of all individuals. As Ellen Petersen states, "You really get people to buy in when they see that these particular competencies help people in your company achieve their goals. They can understand how these behaviors created success, and how people are better off when they're trained and developed with these competencies in mind."

How to Develop a Competency Model for Your Organization

All competency models are based on the concept of identifying what outstanding performers are doing on their jobs that enables them to produce superior results. There are three fundamental components to identifying competencies:

1. Select some of the job's most effective performers.
2. Study what these people do that distinguishes them from their less-effective counterparts.
3. Identify the competencies that account for this difference.

While a core group of competencies are commonly found in leadership models (like those we identified in the last chapter), there is value added in developing unique competency models for individual jobs, job families, and businesses. Competency models are situational and most effective when they directly link to the business strategy. In other words, the more thoroughly the competencies are researched, the more accurate they will be in specifying what success looks like in a given job.

However, developing competency models that are specific to a particular company's strategy, and even more specific to a particular job, is time consuming and resource intensive, whether it's done by an outside consulting firm that specializes in this type of behavioral research or by internal staff that are trained to do this type of work. A variety of methods allow you to develop job-specific or company-specific competency models, and it is useful to weigh the cost/benefit decisions when deciding which approach to take. This chapter shows you the most common methods of developing competencies, along with the pros and cons of each one.

Four key approaches are most frequently used. While different consulting firms label these approaches somewhat differently, they are as follows:

1. Best practices
2. Tailoring best practices
3. Behaviorally researched models
4. Just-noticeable difference scales

Figure 5.1 presents an overview of these approaches. Note that the methods go from least complex (best practices) to most complex (just-noticeable differences).

HOW TO DEVELOP A COMPETENCY MODEL FOR YOUR ORGANIZATION			
APPROACH	KEY STEPS	ADVANTAGES	DISADVANTAGES
Best Practices	o Published Research o Industry Practices	o Good research, easily available o Time and Cost Effective	o Not tailored to specific industry and organizational culture o No employee buy-in
Tailoring Best Practices (Interviews, Focus Group and Card Sort)	o Interviews with Executives and Focus Groups o Utilize a card sort	o Ease of use o Employee involvement and buy-in can be achieved	o Not tailored to specific jobs o Lack of specific accuracy to match to specific positions
Behaviorally Researched Models	o In-depth detailed interviews with outstanding performers in job categories o Sampling of the population	o Tailored specifically to the organization's unique culture and specific success factors of key positions and job families	o Requires significant research o Coordination of effort to be implemented organization wide
Just Noticeable Difference Scales	o Job Evaluation of expected competency requirements for each position	o Tool can be developed to precisely identify job gaps	o Complexity of administration and implementation o Highly trained researchers and in-depth training to be effective

Figure 5.1   How to develop a competency model for your organization.

Approach One: Best Practices

The easiest way to develop competencies is to use what we call off-the-shelf competency models, or best practices, that are readily available in books and other published research. Even the last half of Chapter 4 can be considered a best practices competency model. If your goal is to provide a small group of executives with competency-based feedback and coaching, then any of these off-the-shelf models can get you started.

By using this approach, you are taking advantage of research that has already been done by others. While everyone would like to feel that his own industry and organizational cultures are unique, in fact many models of leadership competencies across industries share a number of common characteristics.

Using existing models enables you to save time and money. If you're going to pay for an outside consultant, for example, and you have a limited budget, you may want to use those resources to focus on coaching rather than researching a unique competency model.

Another advantage is that if you don't have experience working with competencies, you can test their value with a generic, well-validated, empirically proven model that is applied to a small group of people. If it proves to be valuable, you might then decide to tailor the model for a larger application within your organization.

A Case in Point ...

A major university healthcare system called me in to discuss performance management. After meeting with the leadership team several times, it became apparent that one of the obstacles to improving the current management process was the fact that the senior team was uncomfortable giving each other candid feedback. They avoided talking about how their ineffective communication had a debilitating impact on the organization as a whole. I suggested that before they embark on a more extensive organization-wide performance management effort, they first engage in a multirater feedback and coaching process.

Because the team had little prior experience with either competencies or feedback, it made sense to use an off-the-shelf instrument with established norms for effective leadership behaviors. This enabled them to share a common language for giving and receiving feedback. They saved money by using an existing competency model and then bringing in a coach to help them meet their competency goals. Using a best practices model and an outside coach, the team not only improved communication among themselves, but they also improved their communication with the rest of the company's employees.

After the executive team experienced the value of the process, they were eager for a broader organization-wide intervention and were now interested in developing a competency model that was specifically designed to meet the needs of their own organization.

Advantages of this Approach

Companies that have limited resources to spend on consulting can feel comfortable using a proven model, which allows them to put more resources into the direct, hands-on coaching process.

For organizations that have little experience with competencies or multirater feedback, it is often of more value to engage senior management quickly in the process so that they are receiving the benefits of the feedback and coaching. Once they are actively engaged in self-development, they have an enhanced appreciation of how competencies can be useful and hence have more interest in tailoring competency models to drive business strategy.

Disadvantages of this Approach

An off-the-shelf approach cannot capture the nuances that are specific to the organization or to a specific job. At best, a standard competency model can capture 80 percent of a leader's job. While organizations can overvalue their uniqueness, obvious differences in competencies are required in different kinds of business situations. For example, a leader of a fast-growing technology company has different competency requirements than a leader of a conservative utility company looking to preserve market share.

Second, when you use an off-the-shelf product, your leaders have no input into its design and implementation. Therefore, it provides them with limited opportunities to buy into the process. Leaders who are apprehensive or directly resistant to participating in the process can direct their skepticism to the credibility of the competency model upon which they believe they are being judged. The competencies can appear to be less relevant or credible than those in a model that is derived directly from data gathered within your organization.

Approach Two: Tailoring Best Practices

This approach is still based on off-the-shelf best practices instruments but has the advantage of getting greater participation and buy-in to the competencies identified as being most important to your organization. The essence of this approach is involving the organization in prioritizing which competencies are most important for identified positions, using an existing dictionary (or list) of competencies. For example, suppose that you find an off-the-shelf competency model that lists 20 competencies appropriate for leaders across the board. To make this list more appropriate to your organization, you (or an HR staff member or an outside consultant) would call a meeting of your leaders and present them with this challenge: "Here is a list of 20 leadership competencies that successful companies see frequently. Out of these 20, which 8 or 10 are most appropriate for our organization?"

Involving executives directly in gathering these data is important in three respects. First, it is useful to elicit their ideas and their own personal experience about what is important in being a successful leader. This can help the executives focus on which competencies are important now and which will be important in the future for business success. The executives can also identify challenges and trends that may impact the competencies that are required for success.

Second, meeting with the executives early on can help establish the importance of the project to furthering the aims of the organization and can foster their investment in the project's outcome. It also gives them an opportunity to sharpen their thinking about the organization's corporate values and how they expect these values to be translated into measurable behavior.

Finally, these discussions can lay the groundwork for the coaching relationship. Asking someone's opinion on which competencies are most important is inherently flattering and can potentially lower a leader's defenses against dealing with his or her own personal shortcomings.

Another way to tailor best practices is to include employees at other levels of the organization in focus group discussions. These groups include the leaders to be evaluated and their senior managers as well as employees who report to those leaders. Each group could provide a valuable, and perhaps different, perspective on what is required for a leader in your organization.

A Case in Point …

Once the executive team at the previously discussed health-care system went through the initial stages of coaching, they understood the value of tailoring the competency model to their organization. In prior years, the leadership group had already done extensive work in establishing core organizational values that were critical to the future mission of the institution. Now that the executive team had received competency-based coaching, they realized that it was essential to link the values to any future work that addressed leadership development. This was an organization that had spent a lot of time defining institutional values such as teamwork and customer service. They were frustrated as to how to make these values more important to employees at all levels. While the executive team felt that they had done a good job communicating the values, they weren't sure that people were doing anything differently as a result. There were no mechanisms in place to hold people accountable to the values or to measure whether progress was being made.

After experiencing the competency-based coaching process firsthand, the executives now knew that this could be a key tool for breathing life into their corporate values. There were 65 leaders in this organization that would be involved in receiving competency-based 360-degree feedback. Initially we used a diagonal-slice focus group, meaning that we chose ten leaders from a variety of disciplines throughout the healthcare system at different levels of the organization to rank and prioritize the competencies that were required for effective leadership in their organization. That process was so successful that it was expanded to include all 65 leaders to gain the participation and input of everyone involved.

Within a single meeting that lasted only a few hours, we successfully reached consensus on the top eight competencies that were most important and best aligned with the values of the institution. These competencies were now better aligned to the needs of this organization.

Advantages of this Approach

As this case study illustrates, companies can draw on the best of existing research and still tailor the process to the specific challenges faced by their organization. Using a large group process, such as the one described in the case study, can be both cost and time effective and can create excitement and energy for everyone who participates. The competency discussion tends to engage people and call forth an open exchange on the genuine requirements of what it takes to be successful in this organization.

This process requires less time and resources than other approaches that involve more direct research. This is desirable if an organization has an immediate need to begin the coaching effort.

Disadvantages of this Approach

Similar to the disadvantages of using a best practices approach, adding interviews and focus groups to identify and prioritize the most important competencies still does not get to the specifics of what makes individuals in each organization effective leaders. At best, this is a descriptive approach, where key individuals are now providing input. This represents an ascribed level of competency identification. As we all know, when someone asks us what makes us good in our jobs, our answer may be significantly different than what we actually can be observed doing on a day-to-day basis. We tend to be more idealistic when describing our jobs than the reality may allow. The behavioral event interview methodology, described in the next section, can more accurately identify what distinguishes a successful leader in a particular job.

Approach Three: Behaviorally Researched Models

Here is a simple analogy to the two approaches we've discussed so far: In the first scenario, our off-the-shelf product is like a packaged cake mix. Someone has already researched what it takes to make a good-tasting angel food cake, for example. We take the ingredients provided and get a good, although standard, result. In the second approach, we still use the packaged cake mix, but we add or subtract ingredients to suit our specific tastes. This third approach, behaviorally researched models, does away with the packaged mix altogether, and we start the cake from scratch. We are creating our own recipe, based solely on ingredients that fit the tastes and nutritional needs of the people who will be served.

If we wanted to create such a specifically designed cake, we would first conduct polls and interviews that would tell us the kind of cake we want to produce. The behaviorally researched model of competencies begins the same way. It involves a disciplined research methodology, which typically focuses on interviewing executives to probe for specific examples of past on-the-job experiences. Competency models using this approach study top performers in the job and determine *what they actually do* — thereby discovering the interpersonal, problem-solving, and leadership capabilities that lead to success.

This rigorous approach, designed to develop job-specific competencies, is best suited to jobs or job families that are directly linked to business success and where the performance outcomes can be clearly measured. This is true of executive jobs as well as key positions in areas such as sales, marketing, or manufacturing, where the link between effort and profits can be measured and quantified.

This approach involves identifying two sample groups, one of high performers and one of average performers in a specific job. A trained interviewer probes for specific examples using an in-depth interview protocol. The essence of the interview includes specific, detailed examples that demonstrate how an individual conducts himself or herself during critical incidents on the job. The interviews are transcribed, and researchers trained to identify specific behavioral data examine the transcripts to identify patterns of behavior that separate the star from the average performers. Further data can be gathered using surveys and questionnaires and can be administered to a broader sample of the population. The competency model is then derived inductively, based on the data gathered during the interviews together with the knowledge of the organization's mission and strategies.

A Case in Point ...

The president of a manufacturing company wanted to define leadership competencies for management within its Sales Division. He felt strongly that by identifying and defining the factors that contribute to top performance, the company would be able to recruit, promote, and develop outstanding leaders who would then directly increase productivity and profitability. We worked with this group to define competency models at the three senior-most leadership levels. The president of the Sales Division used the competencies both as the foundation for coaching and as the measurement for awarding performance bonuses each year.

Our research indicated that one of the competencies identified for the senior team was "developing others." The president strongly believed in promoting from within and wanted to push responsibility downward. He felt that this would empower the sales force to expand their range of decision-making and free some of management's time for providing strategic direction and developing new business opportunities.

The president used this model in his own coaching and felt that it provided his team with clear direction, not only in what he wanted to accomplish but also in how he expected the team to get results. He told us about one situation in which he tried to make it known to one of his high-performing senior managers that just getting the numbers wasn't enough.

This manager saw himself as a superstar and was achieving results by running roughshod over his people. He often took over the large accounts himself and made sure that he personally closed the deal. His people felt intimidated and defeated and left the company for better jobs when good opportunities came up. This was a classic case of sacrificing the long-term benefits of developing people for the short-term gain of making this year's numbers.

The president focused on coaching this manager on the specific behaviors that are expected in developing others and where he needed to make improvements. The president supported his development by giving this manager the opportunity to receive outside coaching and at the same time tying his bonus potential not only to his sales figures but also to the development of his people.

Advantages of this Approach

The advantage of building a competency model using behavioral research is that it is based on data that show what star performers do at a certain leadership level in a specific role in your organization. This is most useful in roles where the correlation between job performance and financial targets is very clear. So, for example, in a sales division of a pharmaceutical company, if we could identify the competencies that distinguish managers with high-performing territories from managers with territories that are performing at or below target, we could design a model that would predict future success. Using a competency-based coaching process, this model would improve the performance of specific individuals and could be measured in the financial success of the overall sales effort. If future sales managers were selected and developed using this specific model, the investment made in developing the competency model would be small compared to the potential sales volume increase. In a study quoted by Daniel Goleman in *Working with Emotional Intelligence,* Lyle Spencer, president of Spencer Research and Technology, stated that of the salespeople in over 40 Fortune 500 companies, the top 10 percent averaged $6.7 million in sales per person, compared to the norm of $3 million per person for the average performer. Spencer went on to calculate that because the typical annual salary for a salesperson at the time was about $42,000, that meant that the top performers' value added $3.7 million, or about 88 times their salary.

A second advantage of this approach is that it goes beyond espoused theories about what it takes to do a good job and evaluates what performers actually do. For example, it is often mistakenly assumed that a characteristic of senior executives is their charismatic style, typical of a Lee Iacocca or a Jack Welch. Competency research has contradicted this finding and suggests that senior executives of top-performing companies display a compelling modesty; it is drive for company results, rather than a dazzling celebrity leadership style, that propels their company to outperform the competition. In his book *Good to Great: Why Some Companies Make the Leap ... and Others Don't,* Jim Collins defined five levels of leadership hierarchy, with Level Five at the top. "Level-Five leaders embody the paradoxical mix of personal humility and professional will," he writes. "They are ambitious to be sure, but ambitious first for the company and not themselves .... Level-Five leaders display a workmanlike diligence, more plough horse than show horse .... One of the most damaging trends of recent history is the tendency (especially by boards of directors) to select dazzling celebrities and to deselect potential Level-Five leaders ...."

Finally, using a research methodology that is specifically tailored to your organization provides a statistically higher degree of validity and reliability, and it therefore can be used as the foundation for other human resource initiatives that have legal ramifications, such as hiring and performance management.

Disadvantages of this Approach

This approach is resource intensive both in design and implementation. Coaching is frequently sought not just for development but also when a leader is having difficulties or is facing new and unique challenges, such as changing business circumstances. The time to lay the foundation for competency models is not during such a climate of urgency. In these cases, it can be more important to start the coaching process using a best practices competency model of leadership and then revisit competency development when the organization is better prepared to commit to the investment that is required.

Approach Four: Just-Noticeable Difference Scales

In our cake mix analogy, this would be at the Julia Childs level of cooking. The cakes here would include subtle differences only a gourmet would be able to identify. The results, however, would not only be delicious, but they would also be perfectly suited to specific individuals within your organization.

This approach requires the most rigorous methodology and adds a significant level of precision to model-building. Pioneered by David McClelland and Lyle Spencer, Jr. at Hay/McBer, these competency scales were developed to establish not only a set of behaviors but also the level, complexity, and sophistication of the behaviors that are associated with each competency. For example, the scale of interpersonal sensitivity is focused on the characteristic of being able to understand the thoughts and feelings of others. As the scale increases, so does the depth of understanding: from recognizing expressed feelings to reading the feelings behind nonverbal communication to understanding the deeper reasons a person feels a certain way (see Figure 5.2).

The relationships between the levels explain why these are called *just-noticeable differences.* They need not be dramatic differences, only differences that are observable and can be repeated in various contexts.

A Case in Point ...

Aventis Pasteur, a global leader in the vaccine industry, used this approach to develop competency models for all exempt job families in its U.S. division. The division's commitment to

- *Developing Organizational Talent* — The genuine commitment to foster long-term growth and development of employees, with the interest of using their talents for current and future needs of the business.
    1. *Provides Feedback* — Gives specific behavioral feedback on performance on an ongoing basis. Provides specific examples on what was done well and how to improve.
    2. *Addresses Developmental Needs* — Objectively assesses others' strengths and weaknesses. Recommends training or developmental assignments aimed at building strengths and addressing shortcomings.
    3. *Initiates Job-Person Match* — Identifies specific developmental opportunities and matches opportunities with individuals based on both identified strengths and development needs. Consistently puts the right people in the right jobs.
    4. *Provides Long Term Coaching* — Creates and communicates a long-term plan for development of employees. Provides coaching and support to others to provide for their ongoing professional development.
    5. *Creates Leaders* — Systematically builds a talent pool. Selects and grooms key people to assure succession planning.

Figure 5.2   Example: Developing organizational talent.

using this rigorous methodology allowed it to base all its human resource strategies on a competency-based approach. As Catharine Newberry, senior vice president of human resources, put it, "Our people could really understand that having a high level of mastery in a particular competence was the difference between somebody who was really going to be able to do the job the way it should be done, and somebody who would turn in an average performance." Newberry also noted that the specific levels that are built into the competencies allow managers and employees to have clearer conversations about particular things they need to do to improve, without the feelings of judgment and defensiveness that often accompany these kinds of discussions.

Advantages of this Approach

Developing competency scales is of most value for individual contributor positions or high-level executive positions. Models can be constructed that address the unique competency requirements of a specific job or job family — for example, all senior executives — and that identify the tipping point required for success in a given competency. (A *tipping point* is the precise competency level that is required for optimal success in a given position. Developing higher levels of the competency beyond the tipping point does not substantially add to job performance.) Just-noticeable difference scales allow more precision in identifying the level of a competency that is required for a given position in an organization. Coaching can be directed to the specific improvement of key levels of a competency that research has indicated make a difference to job performance.

Disadvantages of this Approach

As with the previous approach, designing and implementing an accurate and reliable competency model based on a just-noticeable difference scale requires trained researchers. If scales are not carefully constructed and tested, issues of reliability surface. Maximizing the value of this type of competency initiative typically requires integration with other human resource systems as well as a sophisticated database support. The level of coordination and administration increases with the level of complexity and number of people and departments in which the competency models are to be used.

Developing competency models is always an investment of time, energy, and resources. Fortunately, options can be chosen according to need, budget, and time constraints, from selecting an off-the-shelf model that represents best practices across a wide range of companies and organizations to developing models that are specific to an industry, company, or unique job or job family. As we have shown, the more specific the competency model, the higher the predictive value in terms of success and the higher the cost in terms of development.

Researching competency models is resource intensive and time consuming. As with other business decisions, the cost/benefit ratio requires evaluation. There always needs to be a balance in the use of resources, be they consulting dollars or internal staff time, between the design of the competency model and the implementation in coaching.

What Competencies Do for Coaching

Competencies give you, as a coach, a perfect starting point. In general, people are more successful when they have specific guidelines to follow. As Ellen Petersen says, "Most people — despite what they may say — are aware of their behaviors, for better or worse. They know when they lose their temper; they know that they don't have enough patience or team spirit. However, they've also gotten by with these behaviors for many years until suddenly, someone comes along and says, 'This is unacceptable.' Now the person is stuck trying to 'undo' a longstanding behavioral pattern.

"But competencies allow you to have concrete discussions and give people standards to measure themselves against. I call it 'constructive confrontation.' Competency models can be very powerful; people can assess their own developmental levels, and have coaches who will work with them on making specific, measurable improvements."

In this chapter, we have reviewed four key approaches to building a leadership competency model that can serve as a foundation for your coaching approach. When you consider which approach is best for your organization, you need to carefully weigh the costs, both in time and resources, with the benefits in role clarity and enhanced productivity. Many of you already have competency models in place.

Built around superior performance	Yes	No
Linked to business strategy and forward thinking	Yes	No
Model supported by validated research	Yes	No
Specifies specific behaviors that can be used to gauge performance	Yes	No
Communicated effectively	Yes	No
Integrated with other Human Resource systems and practices	Yes	No
Cost-benefit analysis to assess best approach	Yes	No

Figure 5.3 Checklist for reviewing leadership competency model readiness for coaching.

This may be a good time to review the impact they have had on your organization and whether you need to do further modification to provide a sufficient foundation for leadership development and coaching. In either case, you can use the checklist in Figure 5.3 to assess how to get started.

References

1. Goleman, D., *Working with Emotional Intelligence,* Bantam Books, New York, 1998, 37.
2. Collins, J., *Good to Great: Why Some Companies Make the Leap ... and Others Don't,* HarperCollins, New York, 2001.

Chapter 6

360-Degree Feedback: What It Is, What It Isn't, and When It Works Best

As a manager, you undoubtedly have your own views on how each of your leaders is performing, and you know their individual strengths and weaknesses. Most managers start coaching from their own personal assessment of how someone is performing in his job. While good coaching certainly includes your own "gut-level" assessment, coaching is more effective when you broaden your perspective beyond your own personal observations. We all bring biases to bear in our perceptions of others, especially when we are someone's boss. However, we can never see how a leader acts when we are not around, when he is interacting with peers, customers, or direct reports. This is where the 360-degree feedback process adds significant value. The data expand our understanding of how others perceive a leader's effectiveness and enable both the leader and his coach to have a more objective perspective.

360-Degree Feedback — What Is It?

Collecting data from multiple sources on how an individual performs and communicating that data back to the leader is the process that we typically refer to as *360-degree feedback*.

The process can be as simple as making a few telephone calls to check on "how Barbara is doing," or it can be a more structured process involving multiple questionnaires, which are completed by the leader, her supervisor, and her direct reports as well as by customers, peers, or others in the workplace.

History of the Use of the 360-Degree Feedback Process

The 360-degree feedback process has its roots in the assessment process and has been used informally for years. From the 1920s through the 1950s, a variety of psychological tests and surveys were developed for the purpose of selection and placement for college entrance exams for military recruitment and business hiring practices. In virtually all of these cases, the purpose of the assessment was to provide the sponsoring organization with data about the person being tested. Rarely was the client being tested shown the results of the testing.

In the 1960s, a breakthrough in sharing the assessment results came from the Peace Corps when the psychologists who were working with the volunteers used surveys that were geared to expand the volunteer's self-knowledge, under the assumption that expanding self-knowledge would help a volunteer better deal with culture change. This was the first time that this type of assessment was done for the primary benefit of the person being assessed.

Today, 360-degree feedback has become increasingly popular for managers at all levels of organizations and has become a core tool of professional development. In this chapter, I examine the fundamental questions that a manager should ask when considering a 360-degree feedback approach as a foundation for coaching senior managers and leaders.

When You Are a Manager: How to Use 360-Degree Feedback

One of the most important functions of 360-degree feedback is to help people get a clear picture of themselves in relation to their peers, their direct reports, and the organization as a whole. People who find themselves in difficult situations can't always identify the root cause of the problem. Getting others' points of view can help the leader make necessary adjustments.

A Case in Point …

Jerry, a senior vice president of sales in a midsize company, called me for coaching when he was frustrated with how to handle declining sales, increased turnover, and low morale in his sales team. He complained that the problem was with his boss, Hal, who would not agree to the incentive plan that he had proposed for his sales force. He felt strongly that this new pay plan would be the answer to his problems and that his boss was just being unreasonable. He wanted to know if I could coach him to be more effective in getting Hal to support his ideas.

When I met with Jerry to get a fuller understanding of the situation, Jerry told me that Hal had managed the sales force directly before being promoted to president of the company and that Hal was still micromanaging the sales function. Jerry felt that his senior people would go around him to Hal when they wanted something that Jerry didn't agree with. As a result, his staff was getting mixed messages, leaving them confused and frustrated.

I told Jerry that to be able to help him, it would be useful to hear how others who were directly involved with sales force issues saw the situation. First, I met with Hal to understand his point of view, which was very different than Jerry's. Hal felt that Jerry was not spending enough time in the field with his people and was not helping them with their concerns and frustrations. That's why Jerry's people were bringing their complaints directly to Hal.

At this point, it became clear that 360-degree feedback would help Jerry understand how he was impacting the organization and how his direct reports felt about his management style. In the survey, we included the opportunity for the respondents to write in comments regarding the issues of morale and productivity.

The results from the interviews and surveys were revealing. Those who reported to Jerry felt that his management style was contributing to their problems. Unlike his boss, Jerry was a "numbers guy." The value of his analytical style was that he was able to provide the sales force with better data regarding projections, trends, and results. However, Jerry was not spending enough time in the field and was more hands-off when it came to handling difficult issues with key customers.

The 360-degree feedback data allowed us to expand Jerry's view of himself and be more realistic about how Hal and his people in the field saw him.

Over the course of a year, Jerry learned to use techniques that improved team cohesion and morale. The sales numbers improved, and Jerry worked on rebuilding his relationship with Hal. As sales increased and turnover decreased, more money was available to pay out to the sales force in bonuses. A year later, Hal had enough confidence in Jerry to broaden his responsibilities to include marketing as well as sales due to his success over the past year.

Advantages of Using a 360-Degree Feedback Approach as the Foundation for Coaching

The 360-degree feedback process is effective for the following reasons:

- It establishes a common frame of reference.
- It provides a benchmark to measure success in the role or changes in behavior.
- It provides a framework for ongoing discussions with your subordinates, supervisor, and peers.
- It reinforces a climate of open communication.

Establishing a Common Frame of Reference

As the previous case in point illustrates, leaders such as Hal and Jerry often view the sources of problems from very different perspectives.

Jerry thought he had established great one-on-one rapport with his direct reports and didn't realize the extent to which they were still bonded to Hal. Hal thought that Jerry was not spending enough time with his direct reports and that incentive pay would not solve the problem. The 360-degree feedback data suggested that the direct reports thought Hal was right; they saw Jerry as a boss who was concerned with the numbers and not them personally. They felt that when they faced customer issues on pricing or shipping, Jerry did nothing to improve the situation. While they were concerned that their pay was not competitive with other firms of their size, they thought that pay inequity was just one of the many issues about which Jerry was not listening to their concerns.

When I reviewed the 360-degree feedback data with Jerry, we were able to understand the situation from a common perspective. As a coach, the data helped me shift Jerry's perspective from blaming his supervisor for his problems to discovering what he could do differently to help his team. I worked with Jerry, not to change his personality, but to build stronger relationships with the sales managers and to stay more in touch with their key customers, anticipating rather than reacting to difficult pricing or shipping issues. As a result, Jerry became a stronger advocate for his people. As Jerry worked more closely with his direct reports, their results improved, and they were more apt to turn to Jerry with their problems. As the sales numbers began to increase, Jerry in turn had more influence with Hal to institute the bonus program he wanted for his people.

Providing a Benchmark to Measure Success in the Role or Changes in Behavior

Using a competency model creates a clear sense of what success should look like at the leadership level in your organization. Especially if your executive team has participated in defining the leadership competencies during the model-building phase, they will be more apt to buy into the results of the 360-degree feedback process.

In Jerry's case, we had worked with him and his peers prior to this coaching assignment to establish the core competencies for the leadership team. All the executives had been interviewed. After we analyzed the data from the interviews, we presented a draft of the model to the executive team for their review and discussion. The model was finalized as a result of this discussion. Jerry had been an integral part of these discussions and had endorsed the competencies required for success. This created a sense of ownership and made the discussion with him about perceived gaps in critical competencies easier for him to accept. He didn't need to be convinced that the perceptions of others were important.

Providing a Framework for Ongoing Discussions with Your Subordinates, Supervisor, and Peers

The goal of coaching is ongoing sustained behavioral change that leads to business success. Rarely does this occur only by a leader having discussions with his manager. Following up on the data usually involves additional dialogue with people who had responded to the questionnaire. Jerry held separate discussions with both his supervisor and his direct reports. He told his reports what he learned from the feedback and asked them to give him relevant examples in the competency areas that were identified for improvement. He told them that he now knew they wanted him to be more available for day-to-day problems and to allow customers and the sales representatives around the country to get to know him. He also worked out an individual strategy with each of the sales managers who worked for him to more actively partner on key customers.

Throughout the year, I continued to coach Jerry and reminded him to recognize the performance improvements as they occurred. I also met periodically with Hal to hear his perspective on whether he saw the changes in Jerry's area he was looking for, and we discussed how to reinforce the positive changes he saw in Jerry. Ultimately, as Jerry built a stronger relationship with Hal, the coaching relationship shifted. My role as the external consultant diminished as Jerry was now more willing to authentically look to Hal for advice and support.

Reinforcing a Climate of Open Communication

By soliciting feedback from others and following up with lessons learned, executives are effective role models for others to give and receive performance feedback in an open, productive manner. By "walking the talk" and using constructive feedback to enhance their own development, executives can set an example for others to follow.

Six Questions to Ask before Beginning the Feedback Process

It is important not to make the mistake of jumping in too fast, taking the "aim, focus, shoot" approach. First, take the time to answer these six critical questions to clarify your expectations and the desired outcomes:

1. Who would benefit from 360-degree feedback?
2. When (if ever) is it not appropriate?
3. How are data gathered?
4. What tools are used?
5. What should I do as a manager, and what should I expect of the consultant?
6. What should I expect as follow-up?

Who Would Benefit from 360-Degree Feedback?

The 360-degree feedback process is often used when leaders are feeling stuck in reaching a higher level of performance, in influencing others in support of their ideas, or in making career decisions. Part of the obstacle is often either a blind spot in self-awareness or a lack of knowledge about how they are perceived by others.

There is a good deal of value in instituting a 360-degree feedback program for your whole executive team, rather than singling out one or two individuals who have been identified as having performance difficulties. If the whole team goes through the process, make sure that you, as their leader, participate as well. This communicates a powerful message to your direct reports that you value learning and are open to feedback. In addition, you are now in a position to be a better coach to your direct reports who have received the feedback. As Tom Dimmick, vice president of human resources at InterMetro said, "The only way to get managers to become good coaches is if they first have been coached themselves."

Furthermore, if teams are going through a 360-degree feedback program together, the data can be aggregated anonymously and confidentially by the coach and shared with the team. This is useful for a leadership team that wants to look at how their patterns of strengths and weaknesses impact both their direct performance and the culture they want to create for the larger organization.

When (If Ever) Is It Not Appropriate?

It only makes sense to use a 360-degree feedback approach when a leader has been on the job long enough to form relationships and have an impact on the organization. This would typically be six months to a year. That does not mean that you should not be informally "taking the temperature" of how things are going from the start. Coaching is very helpful to someone who is just getting started in a new job, but using others' input can be done on a more informal basis.

How Are Data Gathered?

I recommend that when you use a more disciplined process, involving surveys and questionnaires, to assess a leader's abilities on competencies, you don't try to do it alone. Use a coach, someone from your own human resources department who is specifically trained in how to give competency feedback, or an outside consultant. The professional coach can ensure that there is a method to gathering data that reflects performance against the established competencies, analyzing the data, and providing written and verbal feedback to the leaders to identify development needs.

Part of your management job should be to seek information on an ongoing basis from key customers, both internal and external to your organization, on how your people are performing. In many respects, this is an informal 360-degree feedback process. However, it is often of great value for you to go beyond this informal process and use a consultant as an objective third party to gather more formal interview data as well as quantitative data from the use of questionnaires.

A Case in Point ...

Aventis Pasteur has developed a comprehensive program for leadership development using 360-degree feedback and coaching. As Newberry told me in my interview with her:

"From the perspective of real growth and development, the 360-degree feedback that now goes on is allowing us, through the competency model, to give people real feedback from peers and staff that is much more important than the manager's view alone. It is very compelling data from the perspective of the leader. Although the feedback can sometimes be a shock, it is more believable in the eyes of the leader than feedback they usually get from just from their manager."

Catharine goes on to tell a story that illustrates how powerful this process has been at Aventis:

"When someone at a senior level begins to lose his credibility, the organization can be unforgiving. Once public opinion has started in a certain direction, it is very, very difficult to turn around. For example, one of our executives used the authority of his position as a vice president to 'persuade' people that they needed to do something instead of appealing to them on a more factual, reasoned basis. In a collegial environment like the one we have at Aventis Pasteur, people saw this as an abuse of power and did not respond well."

In this case, Aventis hired an external coach to administer 360-degree feedback. The executive took the feedback to heart. He is now doing quarterly follow-ups with his people, and he spends much more time talking to them about issues and less time saying you must do this because "I'm in charge." He worked with his coach to write a detailed development plan in which he identified two people within Aventis Pasteur to be internal mentors. When difficult issues come up, he has a few people to reach out to and say, "I'm wrestling with this problem. This is what I think I want to do about it. What do you think?"

According to Catharine, "The feedback seems to be working. He is approaching people in a more collaborative way and getting better results. I think the next time a promotional opportunity is available, he is going to get it."

What Tools Are Used?

A best practice for using 360-degree feedback as a foundation for coaching is to go beyond using a single measure of leadership performance. In addition to interviews, multiple questionnaires can add to the richness and depth of the data. There are three valuable reasons for using structured questionnaires. First, the quantitative data reveal precise discrepancies between the leader's self-perceptions and how she is perceived by others. This type of gap analysis can be used to target performance-improvement areas for the individual. An additional advantage of using data is that data are compelling to senior executives who are used to dealing with numbers and may discount recommendations for changing their behavior if the recommendations are just based on the opinions of others.

Finally, quantitative data are appropriate for group comparisons. While the individual data are confidential, if team or organizational data have been collected or if industry norms are available, a leader can use those as a basis of comparison. While a variety of surveys are useful, the following sections present some that I use most frequently.

Competency Questionnaires

In selecting a competency questionnaire, make sure that the data will be based on the competencies your organization has identified as being important. While several generic competency questionnaires are on the market, many of them with Internet capability, having a consultant tailor the survey to your organization ensures that people who complete the survey see it as being relevant.

Because competencies provide potential depth of analysis, they can also be difficult to interpret. Look for a data feedback report that is clear and graphically represents patterns of agreement and disagreement among raters. Of particular importance are the level of agreement (1) between self and others (for example, between self and direct reports), (2) within a rating group (for example, all peers should rate the leader's strengths and weaknesses in a similar pattern), and (3) within rating groups (for example, the supervisor's ratings should be compared to those of the direct reports).

How the data are presented and explained enables the leader to understand the facts as well as the implications of the 360-degree feedback. Report formats can vary widely with the specific needs of the situation and the context in which the leader is receiving feedback. Some organizations appreciate a lengthy analysis along with detailed visual displays of the data, while others are looking for a briefer written summary that highlights specific strengths and development needs.

Myers-Briggs Temperament Inventory

The Myers-Briggs Temperament Inventory, one of the most popular models of personality types, is a second instrument that I frequently use to augment the use of a competency profile. Using the Myers-Briggs styles provides a useful comparison to the competency data and gives the leader an added perspective of how preferences influence behavior. While the results of a competency survey evaluate the execution of abilities, skills, and talents, the Myers-Briggs profile sheds light on why the leader prefers some situations over others and how that impacts his performance. For example, one dimension of the Myers-Briggs Temperament Inventory measures the preference for introversion versus extroversion. An introverted leader would tend to become more energized by ideas and reflection, while an extroverted leader becomes engaged through interactions with others. A leader with an introverted profile may also get feedback that he needs to develop his competencies around communicating a compelling vision. In this situation, the coach may be able to identify that the issue is not the fact that the leader lacks the ability to generate an exciting projection of the future but that he is not making the most of communication forums, where he can communicate the vision in a way that builds excitement and commitment to the organization.

Managerial Style

While a competency survey asks questions that are relevant to assessing a manager's style, it is often useful to provide an additional frame of reference to the competency profile. An instrument that I frequently use is a standardized management styles inventory, such as the one published by Hay McBer, which evaluates the effect of an individual's style of management on his coworkers.

This inventory can be given to the participant as well as to his or her direct reports. As such, it is another 360-degree feedback instrument in which a gap analysis can reveal a leader's self-perception compared to how others see her.

Interviews

In gathering 360-degree feedback, the qualitative data gathered through interviews are equally as important. In an interview, the coach can probe areas that can provide rich examples of how the leader being coached can maximize her performance for the organization.

1. How do you define success in your current job?
2. What do you see as challenges in your job? Give me an example.
3. What do you see as the next steps in your career? What will be the nature of the work, and might it be different from what you are doing now?
4. Tell me about a recent work experience that you consider a personal achievement. How were you involved and what did you do?
5. Can you tell me about a time that you seized an opportunity and took the ball and ran with it?
6. Tell me about a situation where you were frustrated or impatient with someone. How did you handle it?
7. Give me an example of where you needed to get others' buy-in and support for your ideas.
8. Describe a situation where your attempts to develop rapport with someone failed. Describe what you did.
9. Give me an example of a recent time when you had difficulty managing someone who reported to you. What was the problem and how did you handle it?
10. How do you develop trust with people? Can you give me an example of where your actions built trust?
11. What do you see as key challenges for your area of the business in the future? What are key problems and how would you go about solving them?

Figure 6.1 Sample interview questions for participants.

In some situations, especially at the most senior levels of an organization, a coach can rely on interviews only to gather relevant data (see Figure 6.1 and and Figure 6.2). A candid interview by the coach, where opinions are solicited in person, can be time efficient and evoke a more in-depth response. The interview typically focuses on work history, values, and professional aspirations as well as on how the leader perceives his managerial strengths and weaknesses.

Questions for Colleagues

In deciding what approach to take in gathering the data, the coach needs to be sensitive to what else is occurring in the organization. For

1. What is your relationship to the participant? (boss, peers, direct reports, or other colleagues)
2. How long have you known this individual and what roles did you work together?
3. Describe this individual's managerial style.
4. Tell me what you see as this individual's strengths and weaknesses. Please give specific examples.
5. What would you consider a major accomplishment of this individual in the last year or two?
6. Can you recall a significant work experience where this individual had to motivate or influence a group of people to do something they were not particularly interested in doing?
7. How does this person handle difficult interpersonal relationships?
8. How does this individual plan and follow through with others to ensure successful completion of projects?
9. What feedback would be important for this person to receive to continue to be successful in the future?
10. As you look to the future, how do you see this person's career evolving at your company?

Figure 6.2   Sample interview questions for colleagues.

example, companies that have just completed an employee opinion survey may be not ready for another series of questionnaires, and employees would be better served by using an interview-only approach.

What Should I Do as a Manager, and What Should I Expect of the Consultant?

Role of the Manager

Once you have decided that you want to introduce a 360-degree feedback process, your first role is to introduce the process and explain why you think it is relevant at this time. If you are using an outside coach, set up a meeting in which you can introduce the coach in a nonthreatening environment. This is a good opportunity to discuss coaching goals and to assure the person being coached of the steps that will be taken to ensure confidentiality.

Even if you are using an outside consultant, it is important for you to stay involved in critical decisions regarding how the process is administered and communicated, both to the participants and to the organization as a whole.

Using the feedback to create behavior change requires your involvement in ongoing coaching. An outside coach can typically only go so far. The coach can help the leader to interpret the data from the 360-degree feedback and design an action plan to address development needs. Once the plan is in place, the coach can continue to provide ongoing support and guidance.

However, even if you have hired a professional outsider to work with your leaders, at some point you need to transition back into the role of coach for long-term follow-up. Renee Booth, president of Leadership Solutions, suggests that when a senior executive has asked the coach to work with one of his direct reports, the final session be a three-way dialogue that includes the outside consultant, the leader being coached, and the executive who initiated the process. The objective of this meeting is to review progress, discuss outstanding issues, and ensure that all parties are in agreement. This is the time to follow up on the leader's development plan, monitor the leader's progress against the plan, provide feedback and guidance to redirect efforts, and assist the leader to engage in developmental opportunities.

Role of the Outside Coach

Coaching for competencies requires that the coach's expertise go beyond the skills that are typically associated with coaching and include a familiarity with the tools and techniques of 360-degree feedback. The coach should provide a rationale for her approach and tools and an overview of the process, including a time line and how the logistics and administration will be managed.

During the initial meeting, the coach should advise participants on appropriate respondent selection. This is useful if it helps the leader make more balanced choices or sensitizes her to political issues that may have been overlooked. Picking only the people who would be most inclined to rate the leader favorably would be of little value and would provide the leader with limited information in planning development actions.

Expect the coach to be able to synthesize the data from a variety of sources and to be able to identify patterns and trends that may go beyond what is obvious. After all, the value of the 360-degree feedback process is to reveal additional perspectives that are not necessarily revealed only through interviews.

A Case in Point ...

A new president of a publishing company, Tonya Jones, was having difficulties pulling together support from her executive team and called me for coaching. During our initial meeting, Tonya told me that she felt that her direct reports were professionally competent but were resentful of her promotion. One of her direct reports was always dragging his heels on project completions, while another was always disagreeing with her advice and complaining that she didn't understand his area. From my perspective as a coach, it seemed that her real agenda was that I "fix" these difficult people who reported to her and make them be more supportive and cooperative with her agenda.

Tonya was interested in my approach to include 360-degree feedback for ongoing coaching of her staff and agreed to be included as a participant. After interviewing Tonya's direct reports, it became obvious that her driving style and "take no prisoners" attitude was a big part of the problem. Tonya used her sarcastic wit as a weapon, and others resented it. While there was some residual anger over her promotion from colleagues who felt equally qualified for the job, the far bigger problem was Tonya's style.

In Tonya's case, I used the three surveys just discussed. The findings reinforced what I learned in interviews with her direct reports. The managerial styles profile showed that her direct reports saw her style as more coercive than she realized. The competency survey pointed to a deficiency in Tonya's interpersonal sensitivity and her ability to understand others' unexpressed feelings. To become more effective, she needed to create more behind-the-scenes buy-in for her ideas and strategies by involving her direct reports earlier in the process.

Using the Myers-Briggs Temperament Inventory as part of the multirater process augmented the other data and showed Tonya that she was a big-picture thinker and enjoyed formulating future plans. Her sense of urgency blindsided her to the need to incorporate her team's energy and views in establishing the vision and course of action required to implement her plans. In her impatience to take action, she was leaving her team out of the decision-making process.

As Tonya's coach, using multiple methods of gathering data gave me enough information to paint a broader picture of Tonya and her leadership techniques. I was able to present a compelling case to Tonya about her strengths as a senior executive as well as the competencies that required some immediate improvement.

The coach should be an expert on the particular competencies profiled and on what development action steps would make sense for each leader. Action planning is a powerful way to assist the leader in integrating the findings from the 360-degree feedback and to realize sustained behavioral change. This planning should address both building on strengths and improving areas requiring development.

What Should I Expect as Follow-Up?

It can be helpful for the coach to observe the leader in action and to redirect the leader when appropriate as he begins to practice new levels of performance in key competencies. The outside coach can often collaborate with the manager to identify special projects or assignments that are tailored to the development needs of the leader; these assignments can be crafted to both accomplish a specific business goal and provide the leader with specific opportunities to develop in the targeted area.

Achieving results is ultimately not in the manager's or the professional coach's hands. The leader has to make the commitment to take the follow-up actions. Soon after receiving the results, the leader should initiate a series of "thank you" meetings with those who answered the questionnaires or were interviewed to provide the 360-degree feedback. It is a good time for the leader to share some of what he learned and to have a dialogue around issues of concern or questions raised by the process.

Six months after the initial feedback, the leader may want to check in with her boss as well as some of the key respondents and direct reports and ask, "How am I doing?" This can be done by the leader or the coach with a few simple questions that are targeted to the areas identified in the development plan. One more option is a short, postcard-type survey consisting of a few targeted questions, which can be administered to the original group of respondents to assess whether they observe positive changes in the areas targeted for development. If the leader knows that there will be follow-up on how he is performing, he is apt to take the 360-degree feedback more seriously and thus achieve the desired sustained behavioral change.

Pitfalls to Avoid in Using 360-Degree Feedback

In many situations, 360-degree feedback has been tried and failed. As a result, those who went through the experience are reluctant to participate again. Our years of experience, supported by literature in the field, shows the following are pitfalls to avoid:

1. The process is only used with leaders who are failing.
2. The feedback instrument does not match the needs of the leader and/or the organization.
3. Data are presented in a confusing manner.
4. Anonymity and confidentiality are questioned.
5. The 360-degree feedback process is not relevant to the leader's goals and values.

Pitfall One: The Process Is Only Used with Leaders Who Are Failing

At times, coaching and 360-degree feedback are recommended for a leader too late in the game, after decision-makers' opinions on a leader's effectiveness have already soured. As Catharine Newbury suggested, it is difficult to turn the perceptions of others around, even if the leader is open to feedback and improving performance. When coaching and 360-degree feedback are used as last-ditch efforts with leaders who are already floundering in their positions, it will be seen as just that — a remedial that probably signifies a leader's eminent demise. When coaching is used extensively in this situation, people who want to build their careers will avoid coaching because of how they think others will view it.

Pitfall Two: The Feedback Instrument Does Not Match the Needs of the Leader and/or the Organization

Choose an instrument that is well constructed and has demonstrated reliability and validity. The domains of the questionnaire items should address the organization's competencies and level of the leader's job. Items that might be appropriate for a first-line supervisor may not be appropriate for a senior leader and vice versa. Ensure that the feedback scales are constructed within sound principles of psychometric research.

Pitfall Three: Data Are Presented in a Confusing Manner

Many methods can be used to present the data in graphic form. We prefer to use an instrument where people can clearly see the difference between their own self-rating and the ratings given by the other rater groups (that is, the supervisor, reports, peers, and customers). Displaying the range as well as the average of the scores for each of these groups also provides useful information.

Pitfall Four: Anonymity and Confidentiality Are Questioned

The use of a 360-degree feedback questionnaire will not be effective if those being asked to rate the leader question the anonymity and confidentiality of the data. With the exception of the supervisor's rating, the feedback from raters should be grouped and averaged to ensure confidentiality. A good feedback instrument does not provide data unless it samples a minimum of three respondents in the category. The perception of confidentiality is important and is enhanced when the data are processed and analyzed by an outside consulting firm that specializes in this type of survey.

Equally important to confidentiality is clarifying, at the beginning of the process, how the data will be shared in the organization. Generally, when 360-degree feedback processes are first introduced in an organization, it is less threatening for a leader if he is the only person to see the data. If the leader has sole control over the data, he does not have to worry about potential negative ramifications of the process on his pay or promotional opportunities. On the other hand, the manager may want to see the data as part of the coaching process. In this case, the manager must be clear about how he will use the information.

Pitfall Five: The 360-Degree Feedback Process Is Not Relevant to the Leader's Goals and Values

We have been in organizations where 360-degree feedback has been used throughout and has had little impact. If people don't use the feedback to improve performance, the program has failed. This can occur when the organizational strategy for using 360-degree feedback is not clearly defined and when individuals go into the process without a connection to their personal goals, values, and career development goals. If individuals are herded through the process without follow-up coaching, the process is unlikely to have a significant impact on behavior or to create organizational change.

A number of years ago, we were asked to redesign a performance management program for a railroad where everyone had recently gone through a program of 360-degree feedback. Because I knew that everyone had received written feedback from others that summarized their development needs, I asked the participants to bring the feedback to the performance management training. Few people showed up at the training with their 360-degree feedback report because individuals had either misplaced it or didn't understand what they had received. When we investigated how the 360-degree feedback was done, we discovered that people had received their feedback report with no coaching or follow-up in understanding how to integrate the findings into improving performance on the job. As a result, the investment the company made in the program had provided little return.

We suggest taking a more individualized approach that answers the question that is on the mind of every leader who goes through the 360-degree feedback process: "What is in it for me?"

Summary

The 360-degree feedback process is a powerful intervention that can provide most leaders with valuable information on current performance and in clarifying where road bumps can occur to hinder future career progression. It provides both the leader and the coach with sound data to develop a useful coaching plan. I recommend using a trained professional to implement the process. Your role as a manager is to stay involved in both the planning and communication. Receiving 360-degree feedback, you will have firsthand knowledge of the process and be more effective in using this as a resource for others on your team.

COACHING
APPLICATIONS

Chapter 7

Using Coaching to Improve Performance

Coaching situations vary and so should your approach. While what I have discussed so far applies across the board, most of your coaching is likely to be in assisting leaders to enhance performance or to take the next steps in their careers. Coaching for performance improvement is a complex issue. This chapter looks at common situations that you will face as a coach, including the following:

- Coaching the leader who is new to the job
- Coaching the leader who is not adapting to change
- Coaching the leader who needs work on relationship building
- Coaching the leader who is not performing up to your expectations
- Coaching the leader who needs to understand how to motivate others

While the situations you may face as a coach have infinite variation, the examples presented in this chapter give you tips that you can apply in other similar situations.

Getting Your Money's Worth: Coaching the Leader Who Is New to the Job

A leader who is new to his job presents an ideal opportunity for coaching. During the first few months in a job, people are excited about the career opportunity, more open to suggestions, and willing to experiment with new behaviors. Someone new to your organization, especially in a leadership role, needs to be integrated into the culture. In Chapter 1, I talked about the outdated "sink or swim" attitude toward leadership development. If you hired this leader from the outside, you have probably invested big dollars in recruiting costs or in the time and energy required of your team to get this new leader on board.

A Case in Point ...

When Ray Welsch, now president of Healthcare Services for Aramark Corporation, was first hired at that company, he came from Johnson & Johnson, a huge corporation. It took him some time, and help from a coach, to realize the differences between the two organizational cultures.

"The environment at Aramark was very different than any-place else I'd ever worked. My history was with a big company that was very organized, very process driven. Aramark is an organization that's really relationship driven, with a higher level of accountability. It was great having my boss, Connie, as a coach and a mentor. She really helped me understand the culture of the organization, the motivation of the organization in terms of growing the business, and the accountabilities you have in a senior leadership role here.

"Early on when I was here and I was in the VP of marketing and sales role, I was talking to Connie about a marketing plan. Connie said, 'Tell me why we need a marketing plan, and what's in it.' So I started into this whole diatribe about marketing strategy and positioning. She listened very patiently, let me get through all of that, and said, 'Now tell me how it relates to the business.' Well, I'm still stuck in the paradigm I had for the other business and as I thought through that, I told her I just didn't know. She said, 'Now you understand why we have this conversation. You're starting at exactly the wrong end for a service business. You're starting at strategy and marketing, when you need to go figure out how the business runs and meet your customers.' It was an enormous awakening for me. It helped me understand the business I was now in, and my place in that business."

Don't neglect your investment in a new leader. Take this person under your wing, build the relationship, and show him how to be successful in your organization. This is a process that takes time. It doesn't occur in a single meeting and cannot later be relegated to human resources.

Promoting from within also has its challenges. While the manager who has been recently promoted may be more familiar with the company culture than a new hire, the promotion is typically based more on his prior performance in his old job than on a clear assessment of how he will perform in the new role. The "Peter Principle," getting promoted to one's level of incompetence, is not completely dead. This occurs more frequently than we would like to think. People who get promoted to leadership roles are typically those who were the best individual contributors or who demonstrated the strongest technical skills. For example, it is often the sales representative who has the highest sales numbers — not necessarily the one who has the most management potential — who gets promoted. The same is true for people with backgrounds in finance, industrial engineering, and market research or in any field where individual contribution is based on specialized knowledge. People often come into their first management job without much preparation in the skills that are required to manage people.

A Case in Point ...

Bart had always been on top of his game as a computer programmer and was excited to have the opportunity to become a manager. He felt that he always had good ideas that seemed to be recognized by senior management, and now he would be able to put his ideas into action as the leader of his department. As soon as he knew he was going to be promoted, he read some of the new management bestsellers that talked about vision and innovation, listened to cassettes on participative management, and attended a few seminars. He felt he was ready to go. He became director of the department in time to head a team that was going to revamp the supply chain process throughout the business. Bart and his managers had high expectations about the productivity improvements that would result from the changes they were proposing.

Six months into the job, Bart seemed to be floundering. Bart's team could not agree on which outside vendor to select, given new budget constraints imposed on them by senior management. What was worse, Bart felt that the people who reported to him resented his promotion and resisted his efforts to exercise his authority in establishing deadlines or criticizing their work. In general, things were not working out the way Bart had intended.

I worked with Bart as his coach over the course of the next year, helping him to differentiate which decisions he needed to involve all the members of his team in and which decisions he should make on his own after getting relevant input. As part of the coaching, I interviewed members of Bart's team, who told me they were impatient with endless meetings and lack of decision-making. They were interpreting Bart's participative style negatively as "analysis paralysis." However, by the end of the year, Bart was making better decisions, was getting more support, and had more influence over senior management. As the team saw him supporting their needs, they began to see Bart as a more effective leader.

How Coaching Helps

Whether the new leader is hired from the outside or promoted from within, having a coach is more easily accepted as an asset at the beginning of a new job. It is too soon to carry the potential stigma that a coach is necessary because a leader's performance isn't measuring up.

When a senior person is hired from the outside, he is often in a hurry to make changes — he feels that he has been brought in to turn things around, contain costs, or expand distribution channels. He may want to prove to you, as his supervisor, that he can be depended on to add value and produce quick results. In a hurry to make his mark on the organization, he may not take the time to get to know his team, what they have accomplished, and what they are proud of. When a leader doesn't take the time to get to know key people in the organization, he can step on a lot of toes in this initial burst of effort, and the resentment this usually causes is difficult to undo.

Coaching Tips ...

- **Take the time to meet with a new leader on a regular basis** — This gives you the opportunity to get to know this individual beyond the requirements of the job. Especially if you are this leader's boss, you need to build a relationship that will encourage him to be open about concerns or frustrations that he is experiencing as he is getting to know the organization. In addition, by helping this leader become more effective in his new role, you get to see your organization through a fresh pair of eyes. Someone new to an organization can often see opportunities for improvement that are not obvious to longer-term veterans.

- **Share your understanding of the politics and about how things get done behind the scenes** — When a leader is new to the company, it is as important to help her get to know the politics of the organization as it is to help her understand the functional requirements of the job. You can help her navigate the political waters and help launch positive relationships with the critical people she needs to work with, both inside and outside of your organization. This involves filling her in on the relevant history and war stories.

- **Remind the new leader to listen more than she talks** — Coach the leader to understand past successes and failures as well as efforts that the team has tried in the past to fix existing problems. Only when the leader takes the time to really understand the people and how decisions have been made in the past can she establish enough trust to build bridges to the future.

- **Focus the leader on getting to know the people who are stakeholders in her success** — These people include key customers, senior management, the board of directors, employees, vendors, and suppliers. As a coach, you can help the new leader understand each stakeholder in terms of how to communicate, what are potential mutual goals, what are likely points of disagreement, and how to handle potential resistance.

Coaching a leader who has been promoted from within your organization should focus on the new role, for example, what it means to be the president and CEO rather than just the VP of marketing. Internal promotions often require that a leader shift priorities, spending more time on the broader strategic goals and less time on day-to-day tactical issues. This may call for coaching the leader on how to simultaneously delegate more effectively and develop his direct reports so that he is better able to handle responsibilities and make decisions more independently.

We all like the kind of work that we are good at and where we can easily be successful. A typical problem for managers who have been promoted from within is micromanaging the technical area that brought them to their current level of success within the organization. The CEO who was the prior head of finance may still have a tendency to second-guess decisions in that division or to unintentionally undermine his replacement when other department heads go around the current vice president of finance with budget exceptions.

If the leader has recently been promoted from within, it is natural for him to bring the biases and perspectives of his prior position. At a higher level of the organization, this may be a more limiting point of view or can be viewed as favoritism. Because making first impressions has lasting effects, getting early feedback about blind spots can help a new leader avoid making early errors that are hard to recover from.

When Using an Outside Coach Makes Sense

If you are the new leader's supervisor, it is not always easy to be objective about your organization. After all, you have built your own history with different people and departments, for better or worse, over a long period of time. Bringing in a coach from the outside can help the leader gather more objective data from his new direct reports, customers, and peers about what is working well and what is not in the organization as well as what these individuals would like to see regarding future directions. Critical stakeholders in the organization may be more open to a coach who is from outside the organization if they think their opinions will be kept confidential.

An external executive coach can also be helpful to a new leader in providing feedback — especially if the leader was promoted internally. The coach can help the leader clarify the competencies that he demonstrated in the past that helped him get the position. What are the competencies that the new leader has to develop to be successful in the new position? What competencies are required for the new job?

An external coach can also offer added value with leaders who have been hired from outside the organization. A new person is frequently hired because an organization does not have an internal candidate with the expertise or breadth of experience required. This typically has less to do with behavioral competencies than with business knowledge, contacts, or prior experience. For this reason, it is less likely that the hiring decision was made with as much knowledge of the individual's potential leadership competencies than can be made for an internal candidate. A coach for a new leader can make a dramatic difference in the individual's ability to hit the ground running and to make an initial contribution that is well received by others with longer tenure in the management group.

Leaders typically bring to a new organization skills and competencies that worked for them in the organization they came from. It is useful for the coach to contact people who the leader worked with in his prior organization (with his permission) for information regarding competency strengths and development needs that shed insight on his management style.

An outside coach is also in a good position to provide an objective perspective for a new leader who must decide who are the "keepers" in the team he has inherited. Some leaders have little latitude in this regard, while others expect that their appointment to the position is a signal to the organization that key positions may be replaced. When the new leader brings in people he has worked with in other companies, it is critical that the new people be effectively integrated into the organization. That goes way beyond the formalities of understanding roles and responsibilities, to addressing the fears and potential resentment of others who have been in the organization for a long time. While a new leader may be busy trying to immediately impact big-picture items such as investor confidence, operational effectiveness, or the bottom line, he may not be aware that an "us versus them" culture is developing. Fractious cliques can become a serious political impediment to getting things done and achieving the business goals.

Finally, an outside coach can help the leader get off to a good start with his team by facilitating a team-building session. When leaders participate in these kinds of meetings early in their tenure, they often find that it saves them time just getting to know everyone. The process that normally takes months can be significantly shortened when a manager is coached through a structured process that identifies what the team needs to know about the manager to be successful and what the manager needs to know about the team. One approach that I use frequently as a coach is to meet with the team without the new manager present and solicit questions and concerns on specific business issues facing the team. I share the collective input with the leader and then facilitate a meeting with both the leader and the team to address those issues and concerns. This provides a relatively safe environment in which to discuss rumors and fears that are on people's minds.

Coaching the Leader Who Is Not Adapting to Change

Remember the boom times of the 1980s? New companies were flourishing, old companies were expanding, and business in general was patting itself on the back. Oh, what a different world we live in now. Over the past 20 years, American corporations have undergone significant changes. The booming economy is no longer booming. Expansion is out; downsizing is in. Mergers and acquisitions are constant and commonplace, and workers are frequently being asked to adapt to new cultures, with more work and fewer resources.

Leaders who are not keeping a pulse on all of these changes will be left behind. As a result, leaders must master the competencies of initiative, political awareness, and strategic thinking. They need to be open to new ideas and to use a level of self-awareness to assess how to adapt their own style to changing circumstances.

A Case in Point …

Maryanne had gained experience in a sales organization where she was one of the few women to get ahead in the

1970s and 1980s. Her outspoken, colorful style got her sales results with her customers, and she was popular with her peers. To be successful in this backslapping culture, you had to be one of the guys. That meant working hard and playing hard. It was a company culture where "zingers" — insults meant to be jokes, sarcasm, and off-color language — communicated performance standards more meaningfully than the annual appraisal.

In this rough-and-tumble sales culture, Maryanne eventually rose to become the first female vice president of sales. It was now the late 1990s, and the corporate culture was changing. The company had merged with a European counterpart that had a much more traditional, "buttoned-down" culture. A greater diversity of younger people now made up the sales force, and they often took offense at some of the zingers that previous employees thought were funny.

At first, Maryanne did well in her new position, but as the European parent company began to take a more active role in managing the Sales Division, there was increased pressure to produce higher sales volume. Maryanne reacted in the way that she had been treated earlier in her career: when the pressure is on, make demands and take no prisoners. This managerial style involved lightly veiled threats to job security and public sarcasm at staff meetings for district managers who were not making their sales expectations.

Maryanne was surprised when her supervisor suggested that she work with an external coach. She viewed the downturn in sales numbers as just part of the ongoing business cycle that would turn around in a number of months if she kept the pressure on the organization. What she didn't realize was that her failure to change her behavior was as much a concern to current management as the results she was getting. The organization had moved beyond Maryanne's management style without her realizing it.

How Coaching Helps

If you are trying to coach a leader who is slow to adapt to change, you must realize that the problem has probably been festering for a while. If you drop a frog into hot water, it will immediately jump out. However, if you place the frog in cool water and gradually increase the temperature, the frog may not notice and may sit there while the water gets hotter. Maryanne was like the frog who boiled to death while the heat slowing increased in the pot. She didn't read or react to the cues in the environment, nor did she realize that she had to adapt her behavior to be successful in this new business climate. Her unwillingness to shift her management style was initially a lack of self-awareness of the impact that she was having on others. After all, this style had always worked for her in the past.

When coaching Maryanne, it was not enough to just show her the facts of her 360-degree feedback questionnaire. When shown the data, she acknowledged that while the feedback was probably true, that was no excuse for others not doing their job. She wasn't willing to change until we told her that senior management had been getting complaints about the way she treated others and that they didn't see her as exemplifying the competencies they had endorsed as part of a company-wide education effort. She needed to see that her career was at stake before she was moved to take action.

Coaching Tips ...

- **Give the leader a wake-up call about how the organization is changing** — Make sure that the leader understands the complexity of the changes required of her. What new results are expected from her in a changing business climate? What impact will this have on the competencies that will be required of her to be successful in the future?

- **Don't be afraid to confront the leader** — Confront her in a compassionate way if you feel that even though others need her to change, she is more comfortable acting the way she always has. Make sure that she fully understands the implications to her own career, to others she is working with, and to the legacy she is leaving the organization. This last implication is especially important for leaders whose excuse for not changing is that they are soon to retire.

- **Use a "coachable moment" while you are working with the leader** — Stop the discussion in the coaching session and point out how you are reacting if the leader is exhibiting the same behavior with you that others are finding counterproductive. For example, some leaders resist change by being the perpetual cynic, dismissing new ideas as being unworkable or portraying other senior management as being unrealistic in their expectations. During the coaching session, it may be appropriate for you to comment if you see any similarities between how the leader behaves with you and the patterns identified in the feedback from others.

Coaching the Leader Who Needs Work on Relationship Building

Some people are outstanding leaders of their team or departments, but they may be hostile or indifferent to building relationships with others. At meetings they may come across to peers as egotistical or as loners, giving little weight to others' priorities. These are leaders who need to develop the competencies of political awareness and relationship building and to see the big picture.

A Case in Point ...

Bertram was a guru in analytical chemistry, with years of experience running big research departments in academics and chemical companies. He had a thick resume, and the awards on his office wall suggested that he was internationally distinguished in his field. Bertram was hired along with a new management team and given free rein for the first few years to revitalize the Chemical Products Division. He had a large budget, as the company was still realizing the profits from its last blockbuster product line. Bertram was also given a lot of latitude to hire his own team. While his superior attitude was not winning him friends with his peers and corporate colleagues, this seemed unimportant to Bertram, who was too busy for such things.

He was caught by surprise when the company merged with another chemical giant and Bertram's results in basic research were given closer scrutiny. As a result of the merger, decisions were made to cut redundant research facilities, projects, and staff.

When Bertram participated in senior meetings that were directed at making these critical decisions, he came across to others as arrogant, uncompromising, and primarily interested in protecting his own people and resources. It was too late in the game to coach Bertram because opinions about him had already hardened. He was labeled as egotistical, not a team player, and unable to see the big picture. Ultimately, Bertram and the company parted ways on less-than-ideal terms.

Leaders who are not team players need to be coached early in their careers, before their track record deludes them into thinking that their success is due to their brilliance alone. Successful leaders can start believing their own press. Special gifts in one area, such as Bertram's intelligence and scientific abilities that resulted in a stellar research and publication record, are often what propel executives into leadership positions. High flyers tend to get promoted frequently and often can leave an assignment before their shortcomings get fully recognized. Someone like Bertram would have benefited from having a coach or a mentor earlier in his career who could have emphasized the importance of building relationships with other important opinion leaders throughout the organization. If Bertram had built that network of support, he would have less likely been caught by surprise when the political winds of the organization shifted.

How Coaching Helps

If you are managing someone who is not good at relationship building, clearly show him how developing relationships can help him reach business goals, both immediately and in the longer term. We live in a culture where "playing politics" frequently has a negative connotation. This can provide a handy excuse for people who are not naturally adept at people skills to begin with. Coaching is an opportunity for you to share your own experiences of how building relationships with a wide network of people has directly contributed to your own success. Sharing experiences can open the door for the leader you are working with to reflect on what he might want to do differently in this regard.

Coaching Tips ...

- **Encourage the leader to network** — Successful leaders get to know a wide range of people (inside and outside of the organization) who may be helpful now and in the future. This might involve asking people to lunch or engaging them at social functions. Getting to know other people on a personal level is as important as understanding the things they are proud of and the challenges they face in their work.
- **Coach the leader on listening skills** — Work on helping the leader improve listening skills, ask reflective rather than challenging questions, and offer support for others' ideas and opinions. As a coach, you may want to observe the leader in critical meetings and offer specific suggestions in these areas based on your observations.
- **Teach the leader to deal with cultural diversity** — In today's international business environment, relationships frequently cross geographic as well as cultural borders. Coaching may involve encouraging a leader to understand the customs of people from a variety of cultural backgrounds. You may need to prod the leader to spend more time on-site to understand how others operate and to learn the nuances that are involved in doing business in a different part of the country or in a foreign country.

Coaching the Leader Who Is Not Performing Up to Your Expectations

Some leaders are just nice guys; they want to please their bosses, get along with their peers, and have a motivated team. The problem is they just don't deliver the results or they get distracted by priorities that are not shared by senior management. How do you coach a leader who is not delivering on the results you expect?

A Case in Point ...

As a vice president of human resources in a retail organization, George knew all about the importance of building an effective team. Even though he was an introverted person, he had learned to spend time with each of his staff and the departments they serviced, discussing their needs and the support that his group could offer. In fact, George's group had been the driver of an employee opinion survey in which all employees had the opportunity to make suggestions to improve the organization. One of the key findings of the survey was that employees wanted the company to change its benefits program to a more flexible approach that was now common in other companies.

The following year, George made designing a new benefits program a personal priority. This involved extensive research of outside vendors, projections of comparative costs, and finally a recommendation that he presented to the president and board of directors. While George's recommendation was enthusiastically accepted, when it came time for his own performance review, George was devastated. The president, his supervisor, had a heart-to-heart talk with George about his disappointing performance for the year. While the president was satisfied with the new employee benefits program, he felt that this was work that George should have delegated to his team instead of spearheading himself. His supervisor told George that he should have spent more time directing the staffing strategy that was required to open three new international facilities. George was criticized for spending too much time in his office on the computer, researching comparative benefits programs, and not enough time traveling to the international operations and participating in planning sessions with the local general managers.

In this case, both George and his supervisor were at fault. One of the keys to getting the results you want is good planning. George and his supervisor never met at the beginning of the year to discuss priorities. George, along with the others on the executive team, had submitted written objectives for their areas at the beginning of the year. In fact, in George's case, his were written objectives for developing both the new benefits program and a staffing plan for the new locations. The problem was that George and his supervisor never met to discuss priorities and to determine where George should focus his efforts.

How Coaching Helps

As a manager, planning for performance is one of the most important coaching sessions you can have. This is an opportunity to set objectives, but even more importantly, to discuss why certain objectives are more important than others. It is not only important for you to communicate your expectations but also to share some of your underlying assumptions about how you expect this person to contribute to the organization's success. This is also the ideal opportunity to talk about the leader's competencies in relation to the objectives for the year. If George's strengths are his analytical abilities, how can this best serve the hands-on approach that George's supervisor would like him to take in guiding the new general managers in their staffing plans? What competencies will George need to develop further to work with the general managers in three very different parts of the world?

Another reason that senior leaders do not fully deliver on results is that they overcommit to begin with. Sometimes in her eagerness to please the boss, a leader may look at her objectives and what she can accomplish through rose-colored glasses. Potential obstacles to success may have been overlooked and contingency plans not put in place. To coach this type of leader, you must understand the underlying reasons for her need to overcommit. (Is she being pulled in too many directions at once? Does she need to learn to say no to some projects?) To really understand how a leader is thinking through these issues and making critical decisions that impact business results, you need to be meeting with the leader on a regular basis, to keep your pulse on how things are going and to provide feedback.

Coaching Tips ...

- **Spend more time setting goals and discussing priorities** — Establish the resources that are required for success, anticipate obstacles, and plan how these obstacles can be overcome. Ask the leader to write her own set of goals and to share them with you. If you are this person's manager, write your own set of goals for this person. In a coaching session, compare your respective goals and discuss the differences. If you think the leader set her goals too high, discuss what resources are required for her to meet these targets. Make sure that the leader has fully anticipated potential obstacles, such as other competing priorities, the budget required, and the cooperation of others as well as other factors that may be out of the leader's direct control. If you think the leader has set goals that are too low, express your confidence in the leader's abilities and ask how you can help the leader achieve a higher target. In either case, if differences persist after the issue has been discussed, explore the possibility of renegotiating the goal to a level that both of you can agree on.
- **Revisit the priorities in ongoing coaching sessions** — Share with the leader you are coaching what you have learned about balancing short- and long-term goals. Give the person specific examples of situations that were challenging for you and how you resolved them. Be mindful of how easy it is to neglect the longer-term strategic priorities because we are so busy getting the day-to-day job done.
- **Simultaneously focus on both the competencies required for success and the business results** — If you are this leader's manager, you will probably have the opportunity throughout the year to observe him in action. Give feedback immediately; don't wait until the formal end-of-the-year review. Connect the dots so that he understands what behavioral issues are impacting his progress toward the business goals.

Coaching the Leader Who Needs to Understand How to Motivate Others

If management were easy, you would be able to tell people what to do, explain how the task was in their interest and that of the business, and expect them to accomplish these tasks. Even when you convince a leader to buy into specific results or competency goals, getting him to take action is not always so easy. Some people always seem to be working below their potential. Others are successful in some assignments while being dismal failures in other tasks that seem to be so similar. It is easy to jump to the conclusion that these people are stubborn, not ambitious, don't care, or are not team players. This is especially true when the typical ways of motivating these lackluster performers — bonuses, career opportunities, and other career perks — have failed.

Motivation is something that comes from within. Your job as a coach is to tap into that inner core of motivation. Your ability to improve performance is enhanced if you have a framework to understand how different people are motivated. In his book written in the 1980s, *Achieving Society,* David McClelland developed a theory of motivation that has stood the test of time and has been useful to me in my work as a coach. He suggests three basic patterns of motivation: achievement, affiliation, and power. He says that while all three motives may be present in an individual, the ones that are dominant have a greater impact on behavior. Understanding what each pattern looks like can help you identify each of them in the people you coach.

Achievement

A leader with a high need for achievement likes to set high goals for himself and others. He gets a great deal of satisfaction from outperforming others and surpassing goals that others set for him. A high achiever typically takes moderate risks and likes to be assured of a successful outcome. You can count on a high achiever to be a good contributor at a senior level in positions such as senior scientist, product development guru, or consultant. These individuals continue to develop their expertise throughout their careers and are sought out as experts in their fields.

The irony is that the outstanding performance demonstrated by high achievers is usually one of the reasons that they are promoted into management. Yet leading others usually involves letting go of some of the nuts and bolts of getting the work done that is so satisfying for someone with a high need to achieve. If this type of manager also has a high power motive, she might do fine. Otherwise, these managers may have difficulty delegating to others, feeling that they could do the job better. Through coaching, leaders can realize that while they have relied on their achievement drive as a strength in the past, it needs to be more balanced as a manager with impacting the results of others.

Affiliation

People with a high affiliation motive enjoy working with others and getting to know the people they work with on a personal basis. They enjoy positions where they can be of help, and they get satisfaction from assisting others reach their goals. You can recognize a leader who is high in this motive if he not only knows a broad range of employees and customers by name but he also knows a good deal about family members, life history, and other details of these people's lives. Leaders with a high need for affiliation tend to enjoy being team leaders and team members. Because they have a high need to be liked, they may avoid conflict even when it is necessary or may overcommit to please others.

Power

People with a high power motivation like to be in leadership roles where they can have a direct impact and influence over others. Unlike someone who is motivated by the need to achieve, someone who is motivated by power does not have to directly accomplish the results himself. He likes to orchestrate events and people to accomplish the desired goals.

People with a high power motive often rise to high levels in business and government. They frequently develop their competencies in political awareness as well as impact and influence, and they use these competencies to advantage. Unfortunately, power can either be for the good of the organization or for the individual's aggrandizement. In the latter case, the leader can come across as manipulative or as a bully.

A Case in Point …

Martin Taylor was a senior-level manager in a large accounting firm. He worked his way up the hierarchy and was admired for his ability to form relationships with large clients that generated high levels of revenue for the firm. He was persuasive and charming with clients but, except for an inner circle of trusted staff, was intimidating and coercive to others. For example, he had a tendency to criticize people openly in meetings when he was dissatisfied, and he used veiled threats, thinly disguised with sarcastic wit, to make his points. When things weren't going his way, he was not beyond out-of-control outbursts that made others run for cover.

Over time, this began to impact Taylor's role as a senior leader. His inability to give other people credit for their ideas or to praise them for their accomplishments led others to not want to work for him. People within the organization who had run-ins with Taylor began to bad-mouth him behind his back. Even clients who were still enamored with Taylor's charm were dissatisfied with the turnover of the project staff members, who were responsible for doing the work. Slowly, his once-glorious career was being sabotaged.

Taylor's direct boss hired a coach for him, hoping that some objective feedback would help correct these problem behaviors. The coach had a number of meetings with Taylor, who at first did not seem to be aware of any problems. After a number of discussions, the coach tapped into Taylor's ambition to be president of the company one day. By clearly identifying his power motive, the coach was able to get Taylor to understand how his behavior was derailing his career ambitions.

The coach began to work with Taylor to use his existing competency strengths — impact and influence, initiative, and directing others — to better advantage by including a broader group in decisions and taking the time to recognize others for their accomplishments. Taylor had glaring competency shortfalls in self-awareness, self-control, and interpersonal awareness. When Taylor began to realize that these competencies were more important than he initially realized, the coach was able to get him to cultivate relationships with people within the firm, giving them some of the same attention and acknowledgment that he usually reserved for his clients.

Understanding what motivates the leader you are coaching can tell you a lot about his managerial style. A leader may rely on a style that worked for him in the past but is out of step with changing circumstances, a new supervisor, or a different culture.

How to Recognize Motivational Profiles

In your first few coaching meetings, spend time getting to know the leader at a deeper level. To appreciate someone's background, it is useful to go beyond the facts on the business resume and understand something about childhood experiences, schooling, achievements, disappointments, and the thinking that went into key life decisions. Once you establish good rapport, the leader is more likely to open up and be candid. As you discuss the past, you can find clues about what motivated him in the choices he made and what may continue to motivate him to this day. Outside interests can also give you valuable data about what is motivational for that person. If Peter once prided himself on being valedictorian of his high school and at age 40 he is still a marathon runner, Peter is most likely a high-achievement individual. Sara, who has a high affiliation motive, today is known as being good with people and enjoys running the United Way campaign. While in college, she was active in her sorority and in a number of student clubs. And then there is Robert, with a high power motive. He was captain of his high school football team and class president in college, and now to no one's surprise, he is running his own company with 19 franchises throughout the country.

Another valuable way to assess someone's motives is to give him a paper-and-pencil test with validated norms such as those offered by Hay/McBer. These tests can give you powerful information but are best used by a trained consultant.

A third way to gather data about what motivates the leader is to ask her to tell you the details of a recent work incident or project that was especially challenging or did not go the way she planned. Probing for both the details of the event and, more importantly, what the leader's role was and what she did and said at critical moments can provide you with information about what motivates her. Questions about what she was thinking and feeling during highly charged moments can also give you insight into her motivation.

Coaching Tips ...

- **Find out more about the leader's background** — Ask questions that tell you what someone was like when she was growing up. Find out what she liked and didn't like about school, and who is someone she admires and why. Ask her to describe her own management style — without making judgments or telling her that you don't agree with her assessment. Listen for the language she uses and the details she provides. Look for the connection between motives and managerial style.

- **Identify the leader's motive profile, and match it to the requirements of the job** — Leaders can be perpetually frustrated or burn out when their personal motivation is not a good match with the leadership situation they are in.

- **Evaluate alternatives if a discrepancy exists** — If you and the leader you are coaching both agree that there is a discrepancy between his motives and what the job requires, identify alternatives. Does the leader want to do the personal development work required to strengthen a motive to better meet the needs of his position? While it difficult to decrease a motive, motivation can be increased. Perhaps you can discuss how to change the job to better meet the needs of the leader's current profile. If neither of these alternatives works, the leader may need to find another job that would be a better match. Finally, you may also suggest activities outside of the job that would allow the leader to meet the needs of his motive profile.

- **Understand that if a leader is interested, a motive can be strengthened** — Motives are patterns of thoughts and behaviors and can be strengthened through observation and practice. For example, if you are coaching a leader who needs to build power motivation, ask him to reflect on how he typically perceives people and situations. Help the leader strategize how he might think about a situation in a new way. Help him see a situation as an influence opportunity, and get him to think about how he might have a bigger impact. Have him observe people who are influential, what do they do, and how they communicate a personal sense of power. Have him analyze what they do behind the scenes to set the stage for the results they are seeking.

All Managers Are Performance-Improvement Coaches

Today's corporate culture calls for continual pressure on raising the performance bar, whether it is increasing corporate earnings, being the first to market a new product, hiring and retaining the best employees, or competing more effectively for customers. Managing the performance of others is core to the job of any leader, and coaching for performance needs to occur frequently and informally on an ongoing basis.

In companies where coaching is not an organizational priority, most managers rely on the performance management process and especially the end-of-the-year appraisal to discuss performance and deliver feedback. Especially at the senior level, there is a tendency to focus on the results achieved in business requirements and spend less time on the leader's competencies and the need to change behavior. In many corporate cultures, "no news is good news." Leaders only hear from their supervisors when there is a problem.

If you are a manager and someone working for you is not getting results, this can become a highly volatile situation because it typically reflects negatively on both of you. The higher the level of the leader who is having performance difficulties, the greater the stakes to both you and the organization as a whole. Instead of taking a coaching approach, the tendency of some managers is to take over the situation, make necessary decisions, and fix the problems. This approach generally provides the opposite result from what was intended. When people feel threatened or criticized, they tend to withdraw support, feel disenfranchised, and perform the job in a nominal way. The discretionary energy they could put into enhancing job performance gets funneled into increased anxiety over job security or anger over the supervisor's behavior or perceived unreasonable demands.

Summary

Coaching for performance is a core part of any manager's job. The five most frequent types of coaching situations are summarized in Figure 7.1.

Coaching Situation	Purpose	Role of the Boss as Coach	Coaching Tips
New Leader— New to the Position	Assure a smooth transition Focus on transition to the new role	Mentor Relationship management Clarify expectations, roles and responsibilities	✓ Meet with a new leader on a regular basis ✓ Share your understanding of the politics ✓ Get the leader to spend time listening to war stories, successes, and things that have been tried in the past ✓ Identify stakeholders important to the leaders success
Not Adapting to Change	Improve self-awareness and organizational awareness	Share experiences Be direct	✓ Give the leader a wake-up call as to how the organization is changing ✓ Confront the leader ✓ Use a real-time coachable moment
Relationship Management	Tie need to build relationships with business goals	Share how you have handled politics	✓ Encourage the leader to network ✓ Build listening skills ✓ Emphasize the need to understand diversity issues
Under Delivers on Results	Help the leader set goals and establish priorities	Set goals and benchmarks Meet to discuss how things are going	✓ Spend more time setting goals and discussing priorities ✓ Revisit the priorities in ongoing coaching sessions ✓ Discuss relationship between goals and competencies ✓ Revisit priorities periodically
Increasing Motivation	Clarify what really motivates this leader	Observation and feedback Assess the match between a persons motives and job requirements	✓ Ask questions that elicit the motivational profile ✓ Identify the leader's motive profile and match the requirements of the job ✓ Evaluate alternatives if a discrepancy exists ✓ Establish a plan for strengthening a motive

Figure 7.1 Coaching situations

Reference

1. McClelland, D., *Achieving Society,* Free Press, New York, 1985.

Chapter 8

Coaching for Career Development

If you are a manager who has developed a relationship of mutual respect with your team, individuals will likely look to you for advice and support for making progress in their careers. This is a special application of the coaching skills we have discussed so far. To offer useful career coaching, you need to explore issues that go beyond the workplace and take into account the whole person, his or her stage in life, family issues, and lifestyle. The first part of this chapter presents a career development model that provides a road map in coaching leaders at critical junctures in their careers; it is what I call the "puzzle of career development." After discussing the model, we apply it to two coaching situations that you may frequently encounter: first, with high-potential junior people on the first few rungs of their management career, and second, with seasoned senior leaders at mid-career crossroads.

Putting the Career Development Puzzle Together

Think of what motivated you to take your own career steps. Our path is often not a straightforward one but rather it takes unexpected twists and turns based on a combination of what we thought we were good at in school, what we learn about ourselves from the experiences we have had, what we have been successful in, and what opportunities came our way. Perhaps we were lucky enough to have a coach or mentor along the way. Maybe life experiences outside the job, such as a new baby or a divorce, have also impacted choices we felt we needed to make about work.

When coaching someone else about his career, it's important to understand that his competency strengths and potential are important, but you also need to learn what is important to that person: what his values are and what needs and concerns he has in balancing work with the rest of his life. Use the career development puzzle (see Figure 8.1) as a model of career decision-making can help you coach others. Make sure you have not overlooked an important piece of the puzzle in considering how personal options impact career ambition.

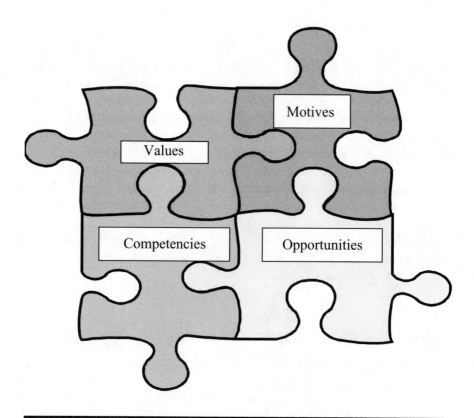

Figure 8.1 Pieces of the career development puzzle.

Values Help Us Prioritize What Is Most Important

Most of us would like to have it all: money, fame, power, and adventure as well as family happiness, economic security, wisdom, and health. With maturity comes an understanding that while we can have a lot of what we want in our lives, probably more than most of us realize, we can't have it all. We make decisions and prioritize what is most important. In fact, those priorities may shift in each stage of our lives. Someone who in her twenties was more interested in challenging assignments and making a professional name for herself, may become more focused on flexibility in balancing life and work when family concerns are added to the mix.

Exploring personal values with the leader you are coaching can provide a powerful foundation for a process of self-discovery. I recommend exploring these issues in your coaching sessions as well as asking the leader to do some "homework" using values clarification exercises (see box) between coaching sessions.

Coaching Tips ...

The following are two good values clarification exercises to use:

■ Take the list of values shown in Figure 8.2, and think about what was important to you in the past, what is important now, and how your values might change in the future. Tell the leader to prioritize five of the listed values in each category. Discuss how and why the leader selected the values, and what issues came up when she was going through this process.

■ Ask the leader to think of herself at retirement age and to write a one- or two-page article that would summarize her career, management philosophy, and contributions to the organizations she was a part of, as it might appear in *Fortune* magazine. Encourage her to use her imagination and to put things in the article even if she is not sure, at this point, how they are going to happen. Discuss the article with her in terms of how strongly it reflects, or fails to reflect, her important values. Ask her to share with you what she was thinking about when writing the article. Did she have trouble imagining the future and if so, why? Where are the gaps between where she is now and where she wants to be?

Values Clarification

Look through the following list of personal values and think about what was important to you in the past and present, and how you anticipate the future. In each column, select five values of highest importance to you at these different life stages. The high values reflect those that give you the *most satisfaction*. Reflect on how your values have changed or stayed the same throughout your lifetime and the impact this has had on prior and current career choices.

Personal Values	Definition	Past	Present	Future
Achievement	Sense of accomplishment, mastery			
Advancement	Promotion			
Excitement	Requiring risk and producing high levels of stimulation and activity			
Fame	Being famous, well known as an expert			
Competitiveness	Engaging in win-lose situations; taking risks			
Teamwork	Working collaboratively with others			
Creativity	Being imaginative, innovative			
Economic security	Steady, adequate income			
Autonomy	Independence and freedom to do one's work			
Family happiness	Maintaining a work and family balance			
Service	Assisting others, improving society			
Friendship	Close relationships with others			
Health	Being physically and mentally well			
Power	Being able to influence the opinions and attitudes of people, to effect change			
				- continued

Figure 8.2 Values clarification exercise.

Personal Values	Definition	Past	Present	Future
Inner harmony	Being at peace with oneself			
Integrity	Honesty, sincerity, being consistent with your ethics			
Participation	Involvement with your peer group, a sense of belonging			
Heritage	Respect for the traditions and the philosophy of the organization			
Professional development	Continuing to learn and expand one's skills and abilities			
Wealth	Making money, getting rich			
Power	Control, authority, influence over others			
Recognition	Respect from others, status			
Geographic preference	Living in the location of one's choice			
Fairness	Being treated with respect by others and being in a workplace that values diversity			
Self respect	Pride, sense of personal identity			
Social consciousness	Contributing to the wellbeing of the community, the environment, or the globe			
Wisdom	Understanding life, discovering knowledge			

Figure 8.2 (continued) Values clarification exercise.

Motives Arouse Us to Action

Understanding motivation is as important in coaching for career development as it is for performance improvement. The more insight a leader can have about what is really important to him, both in terms of values and motives, the more of a genuine commitment he can make to take the actions that directly lead to his goals. People are interested in things such as recognition, being liked, doing something they think is important, or increasing power and influence. No one comes to work and says "I'm really in the mood this morning to write the last version of the report that I'm sending to the board for its review." What he is thinking about is how to get in his supervisor's favor and be in line for a desired promotion, or how to make a contribution and escape too much scrutiny before retirement.

What you can do as a coach is to deeply listen for people's motivations in how they express their aspirations and hopes, and what is really important to them. Is what they describe as being paramount congruent with how they spend their time, both inside and outside the workplace? A gap, or lack of congruency, may be a sign that their values and motives are not aligned. It is not uncommon that when people stop and reflect on where they want to go with their careers, they realize that there can be a conflict between their values and their motives, and that this it what is keeping them mentally stuck and unsure of the next path to pursue.

A Case in Point …

Sally was a vice president of human resources for a division of a major multinational service company. She had an advanced degree in industrial relations from an Ivy League school and always had been on the fast track with her career, working for big companies and quickly assuming positions of greater responsibilities. She liked the challenge of her current position and enjoyed the power that came with orchestrating things behind the scenes. Line managers saw her as someone who could be objective and knowledgeable in resolving labor management disputes and frequently sought her out. Part of the problem, however, was that Sally was frequently on a plane traveling to the company's far-reaching operations, and Sally also felt a responsibility to her two school-age children. Sally was a trusted advisor of senior corporate management, and as the company continued to grow, she was being tapped for positions that would broaden her scope of accountability.

Sally sought out a career coach to help her resolve her ambivalence about where to go with her career. Her coach helped her identify that while leadership positions are typically sought by those with a high need for power, in Sally's case, the leadership position was appealing because of her achievement drive, and in big organizations, one of the ways achievement is recognized is through promotions and higher job titles. Sally was no slacker in the motives of affiliation and power, but those were relatively less dominant in driving Sally's actions and decisions.

Sally took a more introspective look at her own motives in relationship to her personal values. A highly ranked value for her was family happiness, and she was acutely aware of how quickly her children were growing up. After further coaching, it also became clear to Sally that while economic security was important as a value, amassing wealth was far less important. In looking at her motive needs alongside of her values, the personal stress that the corporate travel was creating became apparent.

Sally realized that she didn't need a big paycheck to take care of her family and could give up the prestige of the title of vice president, as long as she maintained her professional contacts and continued to be involved in creative and interesting projects. After the self-reflection that occurred as a result of the coaching, Sally was able to make the decision to leave her corporate career, at least for the time being, in favor of freelance assignments that would give her much greater flexibility to spend more time with her growing family.

As in Sally's case, it is only after looking at someone's motives in relationship to her values that points of friction can be identified. Once the career issues become clearer, it becomes easier to figure out how to resolve them.

Coaching Tips ...

Ask yourself the following questions when coaching:

- What are the underlying motivators for the person I am coaching? Are they in alignment with what she is doing now and what she wants to be doing with her career?
- Are his motives and values consistent, or are they pulling her in different directions?
- Will she need to work on developing any of the three motivational factors (achievement, affiliation, and power) to achieve her career goal?

Competencies for Career Progress Need to Be Identified

Understanding how others perceive the leader's competencies plays as significant a role in career development as it does in performance improvement. However, the focus in career coaching is not only the leader's current capabilities but also his potential. Discover how committed the leader is to work on developing the competencies that may be required for future positions. As a coach, you can help the leader identify competency requirements he needs to be promoted or to expand his role in a new direction.

For example, consider the competency of political awareness. This competency is increasingly important for leadership success and can derail an otherwise successful executive in his career. Disdain or disinterest in organizational politics is a liability and hinders an executive's ability to mobilize support and get ideas implemented. Lack of political awareness directly limits a leader's ability to impact and influence an organization.

A Case in Point ...

One of our clients, Jim, had a high-profile job earlier in his career as a finance director for products development of a toy company. He reported to the senior vice president of sales, who was a hard-charging, "take no prisoners" type of leader. At one critical project review, Jim was asked to provide a financial analysis on potential acquisitions in a meeting with the president of the company and other senior executives. As finance director, Jim had to balance his need to take a hard look at the numbers with supporting his peers on the executive team who were clearly strong advocates of the proposal.

In one unfortunate meeting, he blindsided the vice president of marketing, Donna, with numbers that failed to support the case she was making on a pet project. Jim didn't let her know that there was a problem with the numbers she was presenting prior to the formal meeting with their supervisor. Years later, when Jim was up for a promotion, she had been promoted several times to reach the senior executive rank and was asked her opinion of Jim's potential. She raised vague doubts about Jim's leadership style, and her objections were enough to derail his career.

Jim was taken by surprise by the consequences of an error in judgment that had occurred years ago. It wasn't until he began a process of career coaching and received 360-degree feedback that he was able to see a link between this prior event and the fact that his career in the company seemed to be stymied.

Coaching people on this competency often involves helping them to read their environment and to pick up on signals from others that they may have been ignoring. This involves paying better attention and keeping one's eyes and ears open to relationships and emerging coalitions as well as reflecting on others' motivations.

Coaching a leader on a more complex competency such as political awareness also requires the ability to reframe issues from a perspective that the leader may have not previously considered. When people think about things differently, they usually act differently. For example, in our story about Jim, one of the factors that helped create the misstep was his relationship with Tom, the vice president of sales. Jim thought that he and Tom were personal friends; after all, he was usually invited to the annual Christmas party that was held at Tom's home. Jim paid little attention to the fact that Tom was frequently at odds with Donna, the VP of marketing, and saw her as a competitor for the president's job when he retired. Tom had encouraged Jim to present the numbers at this very public meeting. Jim was naive and never considered that his "friend" would try to manipulate him to further his own ambitions. To help get Jim's career back on track, he needed to learn to view his relationships in the workplace as more complex than he was used to viewing them in other areas of his life.

Coaching Tips ...

- **Shadow the leader and watch him in action** — You can compare your own reaction to situations of the leader you are coaching and see where there are similarities and gaps in perspective.
- **Identify underlying assumptions and beliefs** — These beliefs may have curtailed competency development. For example, Jim's rationale was "I hate playing company politics." Help develop a new frame of reference, and provide ideas on how to get started developing new practices.

Opportunities Need to Be Realistically Assessed

Opportunities are the fourth component of our career development puzzle. You may be coaching someone who has all the values, motives, and competencies to be president of your company. Yet if your company is run by the founding family, for example, it is unlikely that this will be a viable opportunity. However, you can help the leader you are coaching to think outside of the box of existing jobs and roles. By more deeply examining values, motives, and competencies first, you can get a more complete picture of what this leader enjoys doing, is excited about, and wants to learn.

Don't limit your exploration of opportunities to existing jobs and roles. Work with the leader to explore future trends for your company, in the industry, and in the leader's professional field. For example, how will changes in the economy, technology, and globalization impact career opportunities in the future? Organizational change always expands the requirements for talents in some areas while contracting others. Expanding our awareness of these trends gives us valuable information to make decisions and to take actions that can broaden our view of career possibilities.

When coaching a leader for his career advancement, be realistic. Most corporate organizations are still pyramid shaped, and far fewer opportunities exist at the top than at the bottom and in the middle. If you are coaching someone who is already in a leadership position, promotional opportunities may be limited. Coaching may be tricky in this case. You want to be honest, and yet you don't want to demotivate someone who is making a valuable contribution in her current position, but is looking for something more.

Coaching Tips ...

- **Look for opportunities to tackle cross-functional problems** — The opportunities for personal and financial growth often come from being in a position to tackle problems and address issues that cross functional lines. As a leader becomes more adept at managing the interfaces between functional silos, he becomes a more valuable player for his organization.
- **Help the leader develop competencies** — Develop the competencies of political and organization awareness, and understand the social network of decision-makers that both formally and informally impact opportunities for advancement.
- **Strengthen the competency of strategic thinking** — Focus the leader on increasing her awareness of

environmental changes (technological, economic, political, sociocultural, or interpersonal) that will occur in the near future (one to five years), and help her understand how this may impact career opportunities.

■ **Understand how new problems can be opportunities** — New jobs arise all the time in organizations. They often arise because new problems need to be solved. Leaders who can anticipate the issues that the organization is likely to face and are prepared to tackle them can put themselves in a position of career advantage.

Using the overview of the four parts of the career development puzzle (values, motives, competencies, and opportunities), your career-coaching approach can be tailored for people at different points in their careers. While a person's career has many stages, you most frequently encounter two of these as a coach: the leader early in his career who you see as having a high potential and the leader who is at a more advanced stage and may have reached a career plateau.

Coaching the High-Potential Leader

You hired the best and the brightest. Now you must keep them motivated and prepare them to take on greater challenges in the future. Your job is to identify talent and to make sure that your people are getting the experience and exposure they need to assume increasingly higher levels of leadership positions. It is surprising how many high-potential people jump ship for opportunities elsewhere because they feel that no one is looking out for them. By the time they are recruited elsewhere, it is too late. This is especially true for high-potential people who are already at the initial rungs of the managerial ladder. Grooming the next generation of leadership is an important aspect of long-term planning.

Become a Mentor

If you wait for a real go-getter to come to you for a career development discussion, the discussion may become a case of "too little too late."

If the request for this discussion comes out of the blue, it may be a sign that the person is feeling underutilized and already has feelers out in the job market. As a mentor, you can offer perspective, knowledge, and insight to help someone prepare for greater leadership roles within your organization.

Tom Dimmick, the vice president of human resources at InterMetro Industries, a division of Emerson, talked to me about the impact of a mentor who he had earlier in his career. He recalled his mentor as follows: "He had the ability to get people to believe that the conversation they were having with him was the most important thing he could do with his time. Nothing ranked up there with that. He remembered each person as a unique individual, he validated their efforts, and he rewarded their achievements. He punished not their failures but their foolishness. Foolishness got punished; failures got discussed."

Is a mentor the same as a coach? Mentoring is a form of coaching and certainly requires the skills and competencies that we have already discussed. However, a mentor can play an important additional role, and that is as an advocate or sponsor for the leader within your organization. What can often be helpful for leaders in the early stages of their careers is exposure to different senior leaders and different parts of the business as well as opportunities to demonstrate their competencies on high-visibility projects. As a mentor, you can go beyond merely suggesting these as ideas for development and actively open the doors by speaking the leader's praises or suggesting her name when key opportunities arise.

As a leader at InterMetro, Tom Dimmick is now in the position to pass on to others the coaching that he received earlier in his career. He tries to be an advocate for his staff within the company as well as to ensure that he makes the time to be a behind-the-scenes sounding board for their ideas and strategies. Tom said that using a competency approach has become a strong basis for his coaching. Competencies have enabled him to create a common framework with his team to help direct their success at InterMetro. He told us a story about mentoring a direct report who has continued to grow in her career through a series of higher positions throughout the company. As part of his mentoring, he has been trying to maximize her exposure to senior people both within Metro and in the larger parent company, Emerson. As he said, "I can't make her successful, but I can give her opportunities and coach her. She is the one who has to be successful." His approach is not to wait for the formal coaching opportunities but to touch base with her frequently on an informal basis and to offer recognition for small accomplishments as they occur. He wants her to know that she is a valued member of his team and to take the risks that are required to continue to develop her competencies in new situations.

Because developing leaders is so vital to sustaining the success of an organization, coaching high-potential employees should go beyond the discretion of individual managers to become part of a systematic approach to leadership development. Identifying and coaching people for increasing levels of leadership responsibility should be part of every senior manager's accountability.

A Case in Point ...

Beth Rubino, the director of human resources development and training at QVC, has made it her mission to meet the strategic needs of the company for growth by instituting a program that regularly reviews all leadership potential at all levels of management.

"We are always opening new phone and distribution centers, and need to populate these locations with some of our current leadership team. We want to pick the best of the best of the current team to seed the new site, because that is our best shot to build a culture that is going to support us in the long run. In order to do that, we need to get the next level of leaders ready. We need to systematically know who they are, where they are, and that they will they be able to move on.

"The result of this systematic assessment is that we know where our talent is. We know their strengths and how soon they are ready to be promoted. It may be this year or in three years, but we know who has potential and what we have to do to get them ready."

Coaching Tips ...

■ **Sell development assignments** — We learn the most from assignments that have been tough or even stressful. Real development occurs from work we haven't done before or from people with whom it can be difficult to work. Unfortunately, even ambitious people turn down tough assignments because they can seem scary and have some risk. You may need to go the extra distance and convince the person you are coaching to get out of his comfort zone and accept a difficult job that he may not initially see as a good career move. Look for assignments that give the leader opportunities to expand his functional knowledge, increase the complexity or scale of responsibilities, make a shift from staff to line, or require a sizeable increase in the number of people managed.

■ **Be altruistic** — It is difficult for all managers to give up their best people to another manager in a different area of the company. Yet it is critical to development in the early stages of a person's career to get a broad range of experience and exposure to different functional specialties and management styles. This probably means that you are grooming some of your best people to leave you.

■ **Don't lose touch after the person moves on** — The coaches who can have the biggest impact on us are the ones who stay in touch as we venture forward in our careers. When we build these relationships over the course of a lifetime, the relationship continues to evolve and deepen.

Coaching the Leader at Mid-Career

Coaching leaders who have already achieved a string of career successes and are at a career plateau presents a very different challenge. For many leaders, success has always been measured by promotions, salary increases, and higher titles. Now at the top of their organizational pyramid, fewer of these opportunities exist. The chief legal counsel may be doing a brilliant job keeping your company out of litigation but may be yearning for something more. The dilemma is that he is doesn't have the breadth of experience to become the president or CEO. So what is next for him?

Then there are the successful leaders who are blinded by their own success. After all, they have reached a senior leadership level for a reason. Even if they have received feedback that suggested competencies in which they might improve, the results they were able to achieve to this point enabled them to dismiss or discount the feedback. Now, even though your company may have changed around them (with a new set of employees and a business strategy that calls for a new leadership style), their ingrained ways of thinking and behaving make it more difficult to change.

Compounding these issues, many senior leaders who are in their 40s and 50s find that midlife is a time of reflection. After years of striving for success, many of us who are at this stage (and I am one of them) stop and think about what we initially wanted to accomplish with our lives, how much satisfaction we are getting out of what we are currently doing, and what we can do to recharge our batteries and recapture some of the challenge and fun we experienced earlier in our lives and careers. The leader may not be completely aware that this is the issue, but she may express a vague feeling of discontent without a full understanding about its source.

How Coaching Can Help

Senior leaders at this stage of their career engage in the coaching process from a variety of perspectives. Some initiate the process themselves, still hoping for promotional opportunities or searching for what to do next in their career. Others are more in a crisis mode, realizing that their career has come to a standstill, and are unsure about what to do. The four parts of our career development puzzle can provide a map for coaching on these issues. Assessing what the leader wants and how aware he is of his own values, motives, and competencies provides valuable clues for insight into which direction to pursue.

Recognize that part of this reflection may include a deeper search for personal meaning. Questions like "What do I want to do with the rest of my life?" or "What legacy would I like to leave this organization?" touch on profound areas for some. New interests often emerge during midlife that can provide the coach with valuable clues about motives and competencies that have been lying dormant and are waiting to be developed. Personal enthusiasms often extend far beyond the workplace and can include such things as travel, painting, gardening, or becoming a leader in a community organization. These new interests often come from a deeper longing and don't seem logical or sensible at first. In her book *Executive Coaching,* Catherine Fitzgerald states that these interests are often suggestive of psychological shifts that occur in the second half of life. She describes midlife as follows: "It is a time when people begin to get 'inklings, taps on the shoulder' with a subtle but increasingly clear message: 'We're back!'" As a coach, you can be supportive of a leader stepping out of his conventional role and connecting these outside interests to make work life more meaningful.

When to Use an Outside Coach

Because coaching someone at this stage of her career often goes beyond issues focused on job performance, it can be desirable to bring in an external executive coach who has in-depth expertise in the interfaces among psychology, business performance, and adult learning. A leader may prefer someone from outside of the organization to explore how early family history has created beliefs, emotions, and unconscious assumptions that impact her current behavior and approach to the world. An executive coach who is skilled in exploring the impact of underlying motives on competency development can help a leader become more aware of how events from the past still shape the person she is today.

A Case in Point ...

For Jake, high school was painful. Short and not particularly athletic, he was not picked for teams or invited to hang out with the cool kids. Jake was seen as a know-it-all in school, and the combination of his zeal for success and intelligence drove him to be first in his class. He was very competitive and felt pressure to keep up with his older brother, who was both smarter and more socially adept. Jake eventually went into business as his brother was training to be a physician. Jake was aware that his parents were proud of their older son, the doctor, and always felt that he had to prove something in their eyes.

Jake joined a financial consulting company and quickly rose through the ranks to become a partner. He was competitive and successfully went after big accounts. He was very focused and enjoyed the environment of the firm, where success was measured in the clear terms of revenue. Jake knew how to be a winner and enjoyed the recognition for his success.

Because of his track record, Jake was responsible for the revenues of the entire region. In this role, Jake was now measured by the success of others. He was promoted to general manager because management felt that he could teach others how to be more successful by sharing with them how he got results. The problem was that Jake had gotten to where he was by essentially operating alone. While he always had one or two junior people to help with the legwork on his accounts, he treated the other senior people more as competitors than allies.

This lifelong pattern of competing with others was hard to break. When other consultants who now reported to Jake would come to him to share successes, Jake would unconsciously begin to one-up them with stories of his own accomplishments. He turned people off by offering advice before taking the time to understand their problems. This had the impact of distancing them rather than creating a relationship of trust. Jake's group failed to bring in the numbers that were expected of them, and people were complaining about Jake's management style to senior management.

Jake's career came to a crossroads when he was asked to step down as general manager and was no longer a part of the senior management team. Jake knew that his group wasn't successful, but he blamed it on the people that reported to him. He felt that he inherited a group that just wasn't strong enough to deliver the revenue that the company expected.

Coaching Jake needed to go beyond the 360-degree feedback data, which suggested that his team saw him as overbearing, a poor listener, and someone who always had to be right. By exploring childhood experiences and patterns, Jake began to see how the outdated patterns of rationalizations from his childhood were still creating an automatic response to competitive situations.

Jake's insights did not entirely eradicate his behavior but gave him more options to situations that triggered these worn-out responses. He made a career choice to accept another senior-level position that did not have people management responsibility and where he would be a "thought guru" in his area of financial management. Jake also came to the realization that committing time to community activities outside of work gave him more satisfaction than he realized; this was a realm in which he felt more comfortable leading and collaborating with others at this stage of his life.

Expanding Choices

Understanding how the past continues to influence our underlying assumptions about people and how these assumptions create habitual patterns of responding to critical situations is particularly useful in coaching leaders in mid-career. The old behavior usually worked well in some situations; otherwise it would not have been repeated. Jake's fierce competitiveness, for example, gained him recognition both in school and on the job. However, it was dysfunctional when it came to building trust and developing members of his team. When Jake began to understand the origins of this pattern, he could be more objective and understand how others were reacting to him. Jake did not get rid of his competitive streak, but rather he expanded his behavioral options for situations that would have previously elicited an automatic response. The goal of an executive coach is to enable a leader to make a conscious choice of how to respond to situations and how to better align his behavior with the person he aspires to be.

Coaching Tips ...

■ **Encourage reflection** — Encourage the leader to take time out from daily activities to get a new perspective on what is really important to her at this stage of her life. Help her to identify key themes in her life history and to see the implications for future career choices. Discussions that focus on family history and key events can be useful in identifying these patterns. Connect these observations to findings of the 360-degree feedback and to how others currently view the leader's competencies today.

■ **Look for outdated views of self** — Leaders can become stuck because they are wedded to out-of-date images of themselves. Some people make choices in their career, because "that is the kind of person I am." For example, one leader who in his younger days was an ambitious "young Turk" and always received the accolades that go with being the best, may now need to delegate more to others on the team. Part of this change in role requires a reframing of what personal success looks like.

■ **Realistically assess current career options** — Start with what the leader thinks are realistic next steps for his career. Explore his reasons for making changes. Help him connect the dots between where he is now and where he wants to be in retirement. Help him assess his choices in relationship to his competencies, values, and motives. How close is the fit and where are the significant gaps? What other career options exist that he may not have considered?

■ **Help a leader who is not progressing** — When a leader is stuck in making career choices, the problem may be that he does not accurately see himself the way that other people in the organization see him. In that case, the 360-degree feedback process may be helpful. The problem may also be that the leader is conflicted between what he really wants and what he feels he should want. This is another conflict between motives and values. To clarify this conflict, ask the leader about other people who have had a major influence on him in the past, including mentors and peers, and inquire about how those relationships have shaped his career path to this point.

- **Explore outside interests** — Midlife is a time when people become curious and involved in new activities that can give them a renewed sense of energy and vitality. These interests can often give the coach important clues on what is emerging as important for this person and how to use some of this newfound energy in designing a position that would be a more ideal fit.
- **Take risks** — Many senior leaders become insulated within their organization, especially if they have been there for a long period of time. In a quest for security, many people underestimate their own potential and the options that are available to them both inside and outside of their company. If a leader is finding his current position narrow and unfulfilling, it is not inappropriate to explore how to change directions both within and outside of the current organization.

A Pitfall to Avoid

Don't raise midlife issues until you have a good working relationship with the leader and have established your coaching agenda. This topic is not frequently addressed in a business context, and you need substantial credibility with your client to effectively introduce these issues and have them seen as relevant in discussing career issues.

Summary

Providing effective career coaching is important to both the leaders and the future success of your organization. It assures retention of your best people, a succession plan that works, and people who are continuing to grow and develop in their leadership roles. For leaders who would be better served by leaving the organization, it can empower them to make a self-determined exit from the organization and leave on positive terms.

Career coaching uses the same process and tools as coaching for performance, but it takes an increased focus on the person's life history and commitments outside of the workplace. As a manager, you may extend the coaching relationship and become a mentor for this leader and an advocate on her behalf.

An outside coach can be a useful resource to augment the coaching that is done inside the organization. When effective coaching requires a greater depth of knowledge in psychology and adult development, bringing in an executive coach can give the leader a confidential resource with a broader perspective to delve more deeply into midlife issues.

Reference

1. Fitzgerald, C. and Berger, J.G. (editors), *Executive Coaching: Practices and Perspectives,* Davis-Black, Palo Alto, CA, 2002.

Chapter 9

Coaching across the Differences that Separate Us: Bridging the Generation/Gender Gaps

---

You don't need to read this chapter to realize how much the workplace has changed in the last 25 years. Walk through the most traditional of industries, and you can see our multicultural diverse world in action. While some neighborhoods, houses of worship, and private clubs may still be segregated, the workplace has come to reflect the larger world we live in. Men, women, black, white, brown, young, old, Hindu, Muslim, Christian, and Jew all come together under the roof of American commerce.

Perhaps the most obvious difference in today's organizations, one that cuts across many of the other official categories of difference, is age. (It is important to note here that many of these generalizations and descriptions of the generations reflect a middle-class socioeconomic group, although even those born and living in less privileged economic classes tend to reflect similar dynamics.) Many companies today employ four generations of workers and leaders. The first of these generations consists of those born prior to and during World War II. While many in this generation have already retired (or are extremely close to retirement age), there is still a significant number who function as leaders and board members of our largest corporations and government agencies. People such as Donald Rumsfeld and Warren Buffet are examples of those still-vibrant and working contributors. They are, like most others in this category, white males who function within our institutions as wise old warriors.

The second and dominant group, the Baby Boomers, were born between 1946 and 1964. This generation represents the largest block of people moving simultaneously through our society. While this group is more diverse than the first, those in leadership roles are still predominately white and male. Within the subgroup of those born after 1953, there are more women, Asians, Hispanics, and Blacks; however, they still fill proportionally fewer of the senior leadership roles. People in the older portion of this group would be Donald Trump and President Bill Clinton; younger examples include news personality Katie Couric and Apple Computer CEO Steve Jobs.

The third group, named Generation X by the media and the marketing industry, represents people born between 1964 and 1977, with those born in the early 60s just beginning to come into positions of power and influence. It is this generation, born during the Vietnam War and during a time of great social upheaval, that is starting to bring greater diversity to our workplaces. In this generation, men and women equally expect to work for most of their lives. This generation is also known as the "latchkey" generation, because for most of their school-aged lives, their mothers worked outside of the home. Many in this group experienced the upheaval of divorce and the resultant blended families. Given more say and participation in family issues, this group also has a different relationship to money than previous ones. For many years, they suffered under the belief the Baby Boomer generation was going to leave behind great debt and a bankrupt Social Security system. This group witnessed the growing power of Wall Street and started saving for retirement early, and they are significantly more financially savvy than their parents. They also saw the end of the old psychological contract between corporations and employees. This was the unwritten but implicit agreement between employers and employees that reflected the "bargain" made between both parties: employees expect honest compensation, fair treatment, and personal dignity at work, in exchange for giving the corporation personal loyalty and eight hours of quality labor per day. This generation of workers is also the first to feel comfortable with technology and with the changes to our lives and work that have resulted from it.

The fourth and final working generation, called Generation Y, is just now entering the workforce, and it is populated by people born between 1977 and 1994. Born or schooled during a time of relative economic prosperity, this group is optimistic, expects to enjoy work, and hopes to be economically successful while they are young and to retire at an early age. Generation Y, often called the Internet Generation, has never known a time without the personal computer. They embrace technology and see it as paving the road to social and economic prosperity. In my own son, who is in this age bracket, I see how his sense of optimism causes him to underestimate how difficult it is to achieve economic prosperity — it is something he has always taken for granted.

The differences in these generations are about more than just time and space and life experience. In their book *Boomers, Xers, and Other Strangers,* Rick Hicks and Kathy Hicks say, "They're gut-level differences in values that involve a person's beliefs, emotions, and preferences." Value differences are at the core of our inability to see the world from one another's point of view. These value differences influence the way we make and spend money, how we dress, the music we listen to, where we go on vacation, how we spend our free time, and whether we get married before or after we start producing children, and they create conflict between coworkers. It is these value differences, represented by the different generations, that have become a marketer's dream and a manager's nightmare.

Coaching Each Generation

How does all this generational information relate to coaching? Figure 9.1 illustrates some of the differences that each generation brings to the workplace. The critical information in this table is twofold. First, each generational group must be approached somewhat differently, because the values, desires, and work motivations are different. Second, if you as a coach approach a leader only from your own frame of reference or generational perspective, you may have difficulty trying to understand and guide that leader.

The Boomer Coach: Coaching the Next Generation of Leaders

Those of us in the Boomer Generation remember vividly the slogan of our youth: "Don't trust anyone over 30." So we shouldn't be too surprised if the younger leaders being coached today are also wary of taking advice from people who are a decade or two older than they are.

Boomers	Generation X	Generation Y
Community-based	Individualistic	Self reliant
Team focused, interdependence (let's work together on a team)	Team oriented (how I contribute differently from others, work must contribute to the team)	Very team focused (work side by side with energized and energizing co-workers)
Conflict resolution	Conflict management	The more difference the better
Value openness	Value being up-front and outspoken	Bluntly articulate
Empower others, welfare of the group over self	Self-empowered, look to own welfare	Self confident, self and other empowered
NFL — centralized decision making, clear division of labor, do as you are told	NBA — individual contributor, decentralized decision making, little self sacrifice, rebellious	Soccer (choreographed ballet)
Loyalty	Must earn their loyalty	Close bonds of loyalty with those who share their differences and honor their uniqueness
Take action	Self reliant, fiercely take-care-of-self attitude	Casually self reliant, nothing to prove
Workaholics	Work must be fun	Work as a way of life and a source of relationship
Pay dues	Good at change, flexible	Customization
Super moms	Cherish free time, want balanced lives/freedom	Thrill seekers and relationship cravers
Optimistic	Skeptical and cynical	Positive and upbeat
Competitive	Financially savvy	Responsibility junkies
Patient	Demand to be kept informed	Impatient, freedom with boundaries
Believe themselves to be revolutionaries	Comfortable with authority; little or no respect for it unless earned (unimpressed with titles)	Embrace altruism, volunteerism
		-- continued

Figure 9.1   Differences between Generation Xers, Generation Yers, and Boomers.

Boomers	*Generation X*	*Generation Y*
Divorced	Children of divorce	Products of non-nuclear/blended families
Colleagues ran away from their parents (missed having available parents)	Crave time with manager	Seek mentors and wisdom, humor from manager (used to being micromanaged by parents)
Technology only as needed	Comfortable/embrace technology	Masters of the Internet; totally technology driven
Learn to contribute to organization	Learn to build own skills portfolio	Life long learning and exploration
Political correctness	Comfortable with diversity	Pluralistic and highly diverse
Used to the limelight	Tired of waiting for the limelight	Feel already in the limelight, stars in their families
Inner examination, quest for self	What's in it for me?	Search for identity, meaning, and value to community
Critical thinkers	Access to information	Creative
Deferred gratification	Dislike deferred gratification	Today, what is my value, what can I learn, what will you offer me, how will you reward me?
Intellectual arrogance, social immaturity	Powerful achievers	Expect success
Ownership for own work	Learning to improve a resume	Lifelong education
Belonging	Self reliant	Crave connection

Figure 9.1 (continued)   Differences between Generation Xers, Generation Yers, and Boomers.

A Case in Point …

Brenda Whitney was an executive with almost 25 years of experience. She was asked by the human resource group to coach a young product manager from the marketing department, who was not her direct report. Jessica was young, attractive, intelligent, and very opinionated.

After Jessica was a half-hour late for her first session and didn't show up for her next two coaching appointments, Brenda naturally concluded that Jessica was resistant and unwilling to participate in a coaching relationship, and she decided to discuss the situation directly with Jessica. After a number of ignored phone messages, Brenda finally caught Jessica in her office. At first, Jessica denied that she was trying to avoid the coaching relationship. After a few minutes, however, she admitted that she didn't really think she could learn anything from Brenda, because Brenda herself had never worked with the marketing software of this particular project and didn't know the people with whom Jessica worked. Brenda was shocked by this response, as she had spent many years moving up in the marketing organization while coaching and supporting managers who worked for her.

Jessica clearly demonstrated a typical Generation Xer's perspective: "If you can't teach me something I perceive to be immediately relevant to me, I'm not interested." Brenda demonstrated the Boomer perspective and belief that breadth of experience and accomplishment automatically entitle you to respect and credibility.

Coaching Tips ...

- Keep in mind that Gen Xers like Jessica value autonomy and achievement. Start a dialogue by giving a successful younger person a platform to showcase her contributions. Asking her for her ideas can be the first step to creating a meaningful coaching relationship.
- Give the person you are coaching an opportunity to discuss why a particular issue or goal is important to the bigger picture. Make sure that you have a good sense of what is compelling or urgent about the issue at hand. Understanding his passion about the issue helps to connect you to his sense of what is important.

Achievement, Affiliation, and Power

How else are the differences between generations demonstrated? The three primary factors that motivate human action, identified by David McClelland (achievement, affiliation, and power), are still relevant, even if they are expressed differently. Achievement, expressed as "see me as an individual," is critically important to Generation X. Tied to this is the theme of learning and growing myself as a unique sellable commodity. What looks like a short attention span to a Boomer is to a Gen Xer intolerance toward wasting time when he could be learning something new or getting closer to reaching his goals.

Affiliation is also present, but the connection is with the peer group or professional affiliation rather than with the corporation itself. This is a reaction to watching parents and others be discarded by corporations in the downsizing and merger mania of the 80s and early 90s. This affiliative perspective is also tied to wanting a support network to learn and grow with and to use as a reference point to measure one's own success in life.

Coaching Tips ...

- **Provide quick feedback** — While it is generally true that feedback should be specific and immediate, this is doubly true for Generation X. They want their accomplishments acknowledged and course corrected sooner rather than later.
- **Give the Gen Xer control** — Competency development is important to Gen Xers; they are eager to see their own skills and abilities grow. Surround them with your company's development resources: books, courses, special project assignments, etc. But let them set their own plan of action. As a coach, you can certainly offer input and propose ideas, and (if you are also their supervisor) you may have some veto power if their plans are unrealistic. However, Gen Xers like to shape their own destiny and will embark on competency development with more enthusiasm if they feel they are in control.

The Next Next: Coaching Generation Y

For Generation Y, peers are all-important as the primary affiliative group. For many in this generation, friends supersede family as the core of their identity. Even more than Gen X, Generation Y is a product of high divorce rates and blended families (families of choice), and they are the most overscheduled generation yet. In the 60s, it was rare to see a young person with so much as a calendar, while Palm Pilots or Blackberry electronic organizers are standard equipment for much of Generation Y.

It is in the power domain that the differences in the generations are most evident. For Generation Y, position power has little meaning — unless it's their own. Their behavior toward those in power positions is often seen as disrespectful, or even downright rude. Generation Y is impatient with the trappings of power. For them, the base of power is respect and accomplishment. They want power when they accomplish what they set out to do. For many who invested in the dot-com revolution, power was an early reward, even if it was more power than they had the capacity to integrate and use effectively. It took the hiring of older, seasoned Boomers to steer the companies that survived into profitability. One trademark of Generation Y and their ascension to power was the inability to discriminate between the owner of the enterprise and the worker. Clothing and office decor all blended together. It was only in the arena of "toys" that status differences were evident (German sports cars for the founder/owner versus Japanese or American sports cars for the workers).

Coaching Tips ...

- **Understand that TLC goes along way** — Generation Y expects the workplace to have a social dimension. They want to be part of a group, to feel good about each other, and to have team spirit. Work is an important source of relationships and camaraderie. If you are a coaching manager, create events that have a social component, such as lunches, off-site meetings, and softball games, and make sure to include your Gen Y employees.

- **Build competencies through accountability** — Gen Y are leaders who are optimistic and self-confident. They enjoy learning by doing and can develop competencies by being put in demanding situations where they can show what they are made of. Providing ongoing coaching while they are tackling a new challenge can give them an opportunity to reflect on alternative approaches and can provide a venue to discuss obstacles or roadblocks. In these situations, discussing the importance of understanding their own and others' behavior can be a powerful coaching opportunity.

Generation X's orientation toward power is to take control of their own destiny rather than to wait and pay their dues as they ascend the corporate ladder. Like Generation Y, they are also highly suspect of institutions and institutional power. Thus, Generation X is more apt to be a member of the consulting or contractor class of employees or to participate in startup organizations. Wherever they go, they want their power to be based on what they know and can do, power to control their own lives versus control others.

As a coach, working with a leader from Generation X or Y requires a willingness to hold two positions simultaneously. On the one hand, you must listen in a nonjudgmental way to hear the issues from the Gen X or Y point of view. Take the time to learn what she believes is important and what she wants for herself, her career, and her life. On the other hand, if her ideas are counter to the prevailing culture of the organization or have the potential to derail her career, it is up to you to find a way to communicate these harsh realities in a way that can be heard, accepted, and acted upon.

A Case in Point ...

I got a call from a department manager about one of his employees, a young product manager named Sarah who was fairly new to the job and the organization. When I collected data from Sarah's direct reports, I was told that she had an intimidating questioning style, so her people felt like she was interrogating them. When we provided Sarah with this information, she was shocked. Not only did she deny that she was aggressive, she made it clear that she had not been expecting such a negative assessment of her style, and she was not willing to accept it. She kept insisting that her people were at fault for misreading her intentions. From her point of view, her style was not the problem. Eight weeks later, Sarah exhibited her overly aggressive style in a meeting at which the vice president of product development was present, and she was fired. During a follow-up phone call, Sarah still refused to accept her part in creating the problem. She kept saying, "but I don't want to be fired," as though she had any choice in the matter.

Sarah was fired after being given a number of opportunities to adjust her behavior. What stands out from this situation is her whining response, "But I don't want to be fired. I'm not ready to leave this company." After three efforts at explaining to this young woman that the decision was not hers to make, she still could not accept the reality of it. She was accustomed to speaking her mind and controlling her own destiny, and *she* wasn't ready to move on. She did not want to hear that her supervisor was ready for her to do so.

As her coach, I tried repeatedly to demonstrate to her alternative ways of influencing others. Her impatience, outspokenness, and lack of respect for those in authority ultimately derailed her. Her style might have been acceptable in a different new-economy industry, but it didn't fly within her company's more traditional corporate culture, which was one of respecting and honoring tradition and authority.

The typical Gen Xer and Generation Y employee is skeptical of authority. He is typically unimpressed by titles and gives his respect only where he perceives it to be due, according to his belief system. This means based on what the other person has accomplished, not based on the other person's academic credentials or job title.

As children of divorce, Gen Xers and Gen Yers are extremely self-reliant and are skeptical of offers for help. However, they have a great deal of desire to expand their own portfolio of skills and to advance their careers. They are eager to do what it takes to ensure their own marketability. A coach who can help a young leader learn demonstrable skills, experience greater personal effectiveness, and be promoted will find himself or herself busy with others within the organization who desire such assistance.

A Case in Point ...

John, a Generation X manager, was the administrative manager of a building services group. Bright, articulate, and results oriented, he was liked and supported by senior management. However, his work group was unhappy taking orders from a nonengineer and resented having a supervisor who was so much younger than they were. They complained that John was willing to belittle them and their budget requests just to please senior management. During the coaching relationship, we began to realize that John had no clue about how he was perceived or what he was doing to contribute to his own difficulties.

What others saw as self-serving, John saw as simply meeting management expectations. Once John saw the 360-degree feedback data, his eyes were opened and he realized how his group experienced his behavior. He became eager to learn new ways in which he could demonstrate more support for his team while still meeting management's goals. As a result, John's relationship with his group vastly improved. This improvement ultimately led to his being given more challenging assignments by senior management.

As his success grew, John talked about the value of our coaching relationship to his peers, and this led to a number of other coaching relationships within his corporation. My credibility as a coach was established when Gen Xer John started to share his own gains as a result of our work together. From then on, others were willing to explore what can be learned and accomplished in such a relationship.

Patience and perseverance are necessary when working across generations. While you might feel that you have a great deal to offer someone in the coaching relationship, until the leader can see this for himself, the work will be difficult and the relationship tentative. Sometimes it is just a matter of persevering and repeatedly offering a leader a safe place to be or small steps to consider before he is willing to see what can be gained from the coaching process. Given the time constraints most people work under, opportunities to be patient with a leader might be limited. A successful coach needs to come prepared with strategies to quickly bridge the age divide and to overcome the skepticism of Generation Xers and Yers toward anyone outside of their own generational cohort group who claims to be able to help.

A final, critical element is the need for the coach to remain confident about who she is as a coach and what she has learned about how to be successful. Regardless of changes in how business is conducted and how the economy is functioning, the added value of most coaches is the personal understanding that they have gained about the reality of organizational life. Organizations are made up of people and relationships, and every generation of workers needs to understand that their success is tied to their own capacity to develop and maintain relationships, while conducting the business of business.

The Most Obvious Divide of All: Gender Differences

Up to now, this chapter has concentrated on the generation gap. But it would be impossible to write a chapter called "Coaching across the Differences" without mentioning gender. Gender differences, especially in communication style, can subtly but profoundly impact the workplace. General coaching principles can be used successfully with both genders, but differences come into play, many of which arise from the socialization we all have experienced in our Western culture. Coaching is, after all, a helping relationship — and men and women like to ask for and receive help differently.

Tips on Coaching Women

While building trust is important when you coach both men and women, the way you build that trust can vary, depending on the gender of both the coach and the leader being coached. For some coaches, it is easier to build a quick rapport when the leader is the same gender and has common interests or life experiences. For example, when both the coach and the coachee are women, this rapport happens through sharing feelings around similar experiences or establishing an appropriate level of intimacy for a work environment. Or, if the coach can commiserate with the leader's struggles to balance work and family or deal with the challenges of raising children, this often creates a common ground of experience. Topics of conversation that range outside of the workplace and address the needs of the whole person can build trust. Women are particularly tuned into the connection and support that they expect the coaching relationship to provide.

On the other hand, when women coach other women, there can be a level of competitiveness that may not arise when the coach is a male. Often women, especially from Generation X and Y, are frustrated when a woman from the Boomer Generation exhorts them to "pay their dues," demonstrate patience, or otherwise work within the system.

While recently working with a customer call center, we were surprised to find a high degree of tension between these groups of women. Those who had worked for the call center for many years did not understand the impatience and lack of respect they felt from the younger women. The younger women were frustrated with the Baby Boomers' belief that they needed to continue to work within the system, rather than to force the system to change to meet their needs. One Boomer woman finally turned to us and said, "You know what is really sad about all of this? We gave birth to them; we brought them up to believe they could do, have, and say anything they wanted; and now we are angry with them when they tell us how disappointed they are in us and how they see us behave in the workplace."

Coaching women across the generations requires us to call on everything we have learned about relationships and the power of dialogue. Most female leaders in corporations still feel at a disadvantage when climbing to the top of the corporate ladder; however, the way they react to it differs based on their generational experience. Baby Boomer women still need to be encouraged to assume their role as leaders and take action to move into the center; Generation X and Y women must be taught patience and acceptance for the slow pace of change.

Because men have traditionally been raised to be protectors of their family, this familiar socialization can help provide a level of ease if you are a man coaching a woman, as long as you bring perceived credibility to be in an advisory role. Remember all the points we made earlier about taking your time and listening to a leader's underlying fears and concerns. Different problems arise when men coach women. When a woman is describing her feelings about a difficult situation, men are more likely to jump in with suggestions on how to fix the problem. This is often a natural but counterproductive urge to rescue the woman from the problem at hand. It is more effective to hear a woman out, ask questions that allow her to frame her own game plan, and identify her own competency strengths and weaknesses. Not only is this a more productive coaching technique, but it also helps her build her self-reliance as a leader.

While both men and women can take negative feedback personally or feel slighted if they feel they have been excluded from key meetings or decisions, the two genders internalize this information differently. Women tend to personalize negative comments or questions. If her supervisor heatedly asks, "Why were the third-quarter numbers off?" she may hear, "You are incompetent." Because emotions can become infectious, she may respond more negatively or defensively than warranted in the situation. One of my key tenets in coaching women is "Don't take it personally."

Tips on Coaching Men

While no one likes to admit his weaknesses, men seem less willing than women to expose their human flaws. When getting 360-degree feedback data that may portray them in an unflattering way, men can become defensive, intellectualizing the data or challenging the methodology. Using the "best defense is a good offense" strategy, men often deflect discussion of feedback on how others see their behavior by digressing into issues concerning organizational culture or by explaining away the findings by telling me there were problems with the rating sample. (Women don't necessarily like negative feedback either, but they are typically more willing to talk it through until they are comfortable with what to do differently.)

If you think the leader is digressing or intellectualizing, your job is to pull the conversation back and increase his self-awareness. That usually means helping the leader get in touch with his own feelings — a task that many men find discomfiting. When you ask the leader how he is feeling about an important issue, he often responds by telling you what he thinks. I asked one senior male executive I was working with, "How did you feel about not getting the promotion you expected?" He responded by telling me why he thought it wasn't fair and launched into a full analysis about how the selection process was mishandled. While I could infer how he was feeling, he was not fully aware of his own emotions and how his resentment was contaminating his current situation.

The value for any of us, male or female, of getting in touch with our feelings is that it is an essential step to being empathetic with the feelings of others. Only when we have some degree of empathetic understanding can we build the trusting relationships that are essential to taking some level of risk required in many business situations.

Another key difference to recognize when coaching women and men is that while women tune in to the connections with others, men often focus on inequities in status and power. As Deborah Tannen, author of *You Just Don't Understand Me,* notes, "Men are inclined to jockey for power in conversations and assess whether they are in a one-up or one-down position." This is particularly relevant if you are a manager and both you and the leader are male. Men are socialized to see asking for help as a sign of weaknesses, so they are less likely to ask for coaching even when it would be of clear benefit. The onus may be on you as a manager to sell the idea of coaching and to assess who would be a good match as a coach for this individual.

Using Competencies to Lessen Differences

Understanding how differences in age and gender have socialized us all differently increases your flexibility as a coach. When coaching people who are from a different background and experience, you must be able to hold multiple perspectives simultaneously. You need to be aware of the values and expectations that you bring from your own cultural frame of reference, while at the same time being open to seeing the situation from the other person's vantage point. You also need to appreciate the value of the perspective that you bring to the situation. Differences enrich our lives, make the workplace more creative, and expose all of us to the larger world in which we live.

Establishing a relationship of trust with someone who has a different value system or viewpoint on the world is not necessarily easy. When working across generational groups, it can be a struggle to be heard and accepted by younger leaders, especially if they do not see the value in the perspectives that a coach may bring. Just being aware of these differences can make coaching for competencies an easier job.

As human resources expert Jerry Harvey, senior advisor to the president at Sesame Workshop, says, "Competencies cut across all kinds of barriers — ethnic, gender, and generation. When you focus on behaviors, it's easier for people to understand what's expected of them in terms of job performance."

References

1. Hicks, R. and Hicks, K., *Boomers, Xers, and Other Strangers,* Tyndale House Publishers, Wheaton, IL, 1999.
2. Tannen, D., *You Just Don't Understand: Women and Men in Conversation,* HarperCollins, New York, 1990.

Chapter 10

Initiating Coaching as a Strategy and Measuring Coaching Effectiveness

The focus of this book has been on what you can do to coach executives to develop leadership competencies. For the most part, we have looked at the coaching intervention on an ad hoc, case-by-case basis. If the process is as effective as we say it can be, coaching for competencies can become the basis of an organizational strategy. Once a few executives have experienced the power of this approach firsthand, they would be in a better position to commit the money and time to use coaching as a systematic way to develop leaders at all levels of the organization. The first part of this chapter presents an overview of how to implement an organization-wide coaching program.

The second part of the chapter presents our recommendations on practical approaches to the measurement process. Whether you implement coaching on an ad hoc basis or it becomes part of the organizational strategy, measuring the effectiveness of coaching is an important component of realizing your investment of time and resources. An old cliché says that "you get what you measure." Introducing measurement as a core part of the program allows you to continually improve the process in the future.

Expanding Your Coaching Effort to Be Organization-Wide

To be successful, a broad-scale implementation of leadership coaching requires rigorous planning. While there may be a natural tendency to want to just dive in to what seems like an intensely personal process, the effort and time taken in planning in fact make it more likely that coaching directly contributes to business results. Consider each of the following steps before moving to the next one:

- Step One: Prepare the organization
- Step Two: Start with a pilot program
- Step Three: Measure the results of the pilot program
- Step Four: Communicate broadly
- Step Five: Implement on a broad scale
- Step Six: Measure the final results

Step One: Prepare the Organization

Whether you are implementing coaching on a case-by-case basis or for a broader-scale implementation, you need to be clear about whether your organization's culture can support the coaching initiative. If the senior team is to give frank opinions through a 360-degree feedback process, the culture must be one where candid and honest feedback is valued. Is asking for help by leaders a sign of strength in your company? Are competencies being used in the organization, and if so, are they well understood and accepted? If the answer to either of these questions is no, you may have to do more preliminary work before embarking on a large coaching initiative — for example, starting with a pilot program.

Step Two: Start with a Pilot Program

You can test the waters by starting with a pilot program of coaching for a select group of senior executives. While conducting the pilot program, you can simultaneously address any issues that would create a more supportive environment for a broader coaching initiative. As managers begin to value coaching and develop skills, more leaders will naturally incorporate coaching in their day-to-day management agendas. However, as executive coaches are brought in to augment the coaching that is done by line managers, the process becomes more formalized. Questions such as "Who manages the outside coaches?" (typically either human resources or line management) or "What is the criteria for receiving an executive coach?" need to be resolved at this point.

If you are implementing the pilot program as a test for broader-scale implementation, select participants with the end goal in mind. Include people who are opinion leaders for the company; they will potentially become allies should you decide to recommend the program for broader implementation.

Step Three: Measure the Results of the Pilot Program

Starting with a small group of executives and measuring the results can provide you with valuable information about whether expanding this effort will support the organization's mission, strategy, and goals. Later in this chapter, we discuss particular methods that allow you to measure the effectiveness of coaching at this initial stage.

Step Four: Communicate Broadly

As we discussed in Chapter 1, competencies have become popular in recent years because they help create a common language and company culture. Starting a coaching program should also be considered in terms of the message that you want to send to the leaders being coached and to the organization as a whole. For example, you may want to introduce coaching to ensure that leadership is prepared to face a more competitive marketplace, which requires your organization to become more flexible and resilient. If that is the case, make sure that you communicate this message clearly. This communication serves to reinforce the organization's strategy while ensuring that all employees understand the reason that management is committing resources to the coaching program. Communication from management regarding what you hope to accomplish in the coaching program can serve to build trust and encourage leaders to participate in the program, potentially as either coaches or coachees.

Step Five: Implement on a Broad Scale

When considering implementing coaching as an organizational strategy, consider the following questions:

What business goal is the program is trying to achieve?

- How is coaching intended to promote business results?
- What messages do we want to send by embarking on a coaching program?

How are competency models currently being used in the organization?

- Are leadership competency models already in place? If so, are they accepted, up to date, and being used to guide leadership behavior?
- How do existing competency models integrate into other management initiatives (that is, selection, succession planning performance management, and career development)?
- How should coaching be integrated with other competency-based organizational initiatives?

Who will be coached?

- How are leaders or potential leaders selected for the program?
- Is the program mandatory or voluntary?
- Who decides if executive coaching is the best solution?

Who will be the pool of coaches?

- What are the qualifications or requirements for being a coach?
- How many coaches are needed for your organization?
- If internal coaches will be used, how will they be selected?
- How will internal coaches be recognized for their contribution?
- If external executive coaches are used, how will they be selected?

How will coaches be trained?

- What are the training requirements if internal coaches are used?
- How will you bring external coaches up to speed regarding your company culture and the competencies required for leadership success?

How will coaches be matched with executives?

- How will you match individual needs of leaders to the right coach?
- How will you include the leader in the selection of the coach?

How will you ensure that the coaching engagement stays on track?

- How will you expect the coach to check on progress toward the development goals?
- When the coach is someone other than the leader's immediate manager, how should the manager be included in the process?
- What information will be tracked and monitored, and what information is confidential? How will the collected information be used?

What logistics are important to the success of the program?

- How often do you expect the coach to meet with the participant?
- Should the meetings be face to face, or can they be by telephone?
- How long will the coaching assignment last?
- What is the budget for the program?

Step Six: Measure the Final Results

The final consideration, whether you are coaching on a case-by-case basis or are looking to broaden the approach across the organization, is the issue of how you are going to measure success. While measurement is the final issue we are going to consider, you should not wait until the end of your coaching initiative to plan how you are going to measure results. You will reap the greatest reward from the coaching effort if measurement is considered early in the planning process.

Measuring the Value of Coaching

Once a coaching program is put in place, how do you know if it's justifying its cost? How do you know which parts of the program are working well and which are not working so well? What should be changing going forward? If the organization has begun a coaching program with a few key leaders, should it be expanded?

Principles of Organizational Measurement

The principles of organizational measurement are as follows:

- Begin at the beginning.
- Partner with others.
- Measure what matters for competency development, and only what matters.
- Use a control group.
- Deliver in real time.
- Collaborate with experts to collect the data.
- See the "whole elephant."
- Be efficient.
- Own the results.

Begin at the Beginning

If you are the senior executive who is sponsoring coaching for yourself or for others in the organization, you need to know from the start what you want to get out of the initiative. This knowledge achieves two things:

1. It helps those doing the coaching and those being coached focus on achieving the results that are desired by the organization.
2. It avoids a common pitfall of coaching initiatives, which is satisfying the individual being coached without directly tying the improvement in competencies to achieving organizational goals.

Coaching Tips ...

The following are specific questions that you should ask before starting a coaching initiative in your organization:

- What do you want to accomplish through coaching for the individual, the team, and the organization as a whole?
- What will look different to you if the coaching effort is successful?
- What are your expectations about time frames, the coach's availability, and the fees if an outside executive coach is used?
- What specific leadership competencies are you trying to develop in individuals?
- If you are going to do the coaching yourself, what challenges or obstacles might present a problem, and how are you prepared to deal with these obstacles?

Partner with Others

Partner with everyone who will be interested in the value of the coaching process to the organization. If there are external executive coaches involved, make them allies in designing the coaching evaluation process. Remember that coaches are people too. If the external coaches are involved in the measurement process, they feel less threatened by being evaluated on their work and more eager to use the results to improve their services. Involve the leaders who are being coached and the people who they impact.

Turn relationships into active collaborations. The relationships should be wide (involve many different groups), deep (encourage involvement in measurement), and ongoing. Senior executives must be involved. This kind of relationship building helps the line organization own the measurement and, over time, take over for HR and the external consultants. It also enhances the credibility of the results.

Measure What Matters for Competency Development, and Only What Matters

Capture the key drivers of the competency development system — be they demonstrated attitudes, skills, or behaviors — with the measurement. If you have identified two or three specific competency behaviors that you are focusing on in the coaching, design a way to measure whether progress is being made. While I recommend that a full 360-degree feedback process be given periodically (every 18 months to 2 years would be ideal) to measure whether the competencies you are working on are being developed, you only need to collect data on those specific competencies.

A Case in Point ...

The University of California, San Diego healthcare system includes two academic teaching hospitals, a 210-member faculty medical group, and other auxiliary healthcare entities. It has faced challenges on all fronts in the past decade, resulting in a strong emphasis in cost containment while trying to enhance the quality of service and care. Sumiyo Kastelic, UCSD Medical Center's CEO, instituted an employee opinion survey in 2000 to ascertain how employees felt about essential areas that impact the organization's culture and climate. An important area that emerged was a concern over manager and employee relations.

Because of the survey findings, UCSD Healthcare instituted several programs to include individual executive coaching and leadership training at all managerial and supervisory levels. I helped UCSD design a 360-degree feedback program and individual coaching as part of their development. When employees were resurveyed in 2002, two questions were included to determine whether the coaching and development experiences had made a difference in attitudes toward management and the organization. Employees were asked to respond to both whether they had received leadership training or whether the person they reported to received leadership development.

The results were dramatic. There was a strong correlation between a "yes" response to either question, and the results on ALL of the other questionnaire items including questions on trust in management and confidence in the organization's future success. For example, respondents who reported that their boss had participated in the 360-degree feedback also rated the item reflecting "respect for leadership" higher than respondents whose bosses had not received 360-degree feedback. In the same fashion, the survey sample who reported that they personally had participated in 360-degree feedback also rated the same item, "respect for leadership," higher. This suggests a correlation between increased respect for management and participation in the organization's leadership development effort.

Coaching Tips ...

What gets measured, gets done. One way to evaluate whether change has taken place is to resurvey respondents to the 360-degree feedback survey 6 to 8 months after the leader has received the feedback and has had ongoing coaching. This time, include in the survey only the two or three specific items that the leader has targeted for development. This can be done on a postcard or in a brief one-page e-mail. Once again, you must collect the data anonymously and confidentially.

An example of a mini-survey that can be used as follow-up measurement is shown in Figure 10.1.

Use a Control Group

To evaluate the effectiveness of coaching, you need to compare the degree of sustained behavioral change in leaders who had received coaching with those that had not. One way to demonstrate the effectiveness of coaching in your organization would be to provide a group of executives with 360-degree feedback on their leadership competencies. Give half the group follow-up coaching, and allow the second half to work on their professional development on their own. After six to eight months, use the previously mentioned mini-survey approach and look at the aggregate findings of the two groups. If the coaching was effective, the group that received follow-up coaching should demonstrate more significant results in the degree of improvement on targeted competencies as measured by those they work with.

Follow-up Survey to 360-Degree Feedback

❖ Since the survey, has this person communicated with you on how they are going to develop leadership competencies?
— Yes
— No

❖ Do you think this person has become a more effective leader in the past several months?
▪ Yes
▪ No

Original 360-Degree Survey Items

Please rate the extent to which this person has increased/decreased their effectiveness in the following areas over the past several months:

▪ Builds behind the scenes support for ideas.
▪ More effective
▪ No Change
▪ Less Effective

▪ Takes responsibility for outcomes instead of blaming others.
▪ More Effective
▪ No Change
▪ Less Effective

Figure 10.1   Survey used for post-360-degree feedback evaluation.

Deliver in Real Time

Survey results should be analyzed and disseminated in days rather than weeks or months. The measurement can often increase the momentum of the coaching initiative, but only if the information is available soon enough for appropriate decisions about continuing the coaching initiative to be made.

Collaborate with Experts to Collect the Data

To keep the process honest, maintain confidentiality and employ statistical processes that are most appropriate for the analysis. It is often worthwhile to employ a consultant with a measurement background to collect and analyze the data.

A situation will inevitably develop in which something must be said that makes people uncomfortable. Be clear about the parameters of aggregate results that will achieve the organization's objectives, keeping in mind the need to maintain confidentiality at the individual level. Achieving the balance between objectivity and advocacy is challenging, crucial, and ever-changing. It is most useful to have discussions about this balance when planning how coaching will be measured.

See the "Whole Elephant"

The value of multiple of perspectives was discussed in Chapter 6 in relation to 360-degree feedback. This principle is elegantly articulated by psychologist Robert Ornstein in his book *The Psychology of Consciousness:*

> Each person standing at one part of the elephant can make his own limited, analytic assessment of the situation, but we do not obtain an elephant by adding 'scaly,' 'long and soft,' 'massive and cylindrical' together in any conceivable proportion. Without the development of an overall perspective, we remain lost in our individual investigations. Such a perspective is a province of another mode of knowledge, and cannot be achieved in the same way that individual parts are explored. It does not arise out of a linear sum of independent observations.

Coaching does not occur in a vacuum. Business conditions, company politics, and culture can all impact the success of coaching leaders to achieve sustainable results. It is easy to be successful when things are looking up and much more difficult when conditions sour. Therefore, it is even more important that the measurement process take into account factors that are within the control of the coach and the leader being coached as well as the factors that are outside of their control.

Be Efficient

Consider cost and effort in the measurement plan. Take advantage of all the available information technology within the company to plan, implement, and disseminate the results of the assessment.

Own the Results

Be very active in what happens to the measurement information after it is collected. Create dialogue on the results widely across the system.

In the initial planning for a coaching program, a plan for following up the measurement data must be developed, and this plan must be implemented when the measurement data become available. There will be results on the value of the program and diagnostic data on what is working and what is problematic about the program. At the very least, the results should be communicated in an appropriate way.

The Kirkpatrick's Levels Framework

Just as tried-and-true 360-degree feedback programs exist, there are also previously tested measurement methods. One well-known method for evaluating organizational initiatives is Donald Kirkpatrick's levels framework. Although the framework is explicitly designed for evaluating training programs, there is a natural adaptation of the framework to human resource development (HRD) programs, including coaching for leadership competencies.

Kirkpatrick's Four Levels

Kirkpatrick's four levels are as follows:

- **Level 1** — What is the reaction to the coaching, by both coaches and participants?
- **Level 2** — What has been learned?
- **Level 3** — How have behaviors changed?
- **Level 4** — Are the behavioral changes of value to the company?

Kirkpatrick's system contains the following operating principles:

- The levels are cumulative, that is, each level builds on the earlier ones. For example, to measure at Level 3 (behavior change), you must first measure at Levels 1 and 2.
- The higher you go, the more difficult and resource-intensive the measurement. Level 1 measurement may occur right after the experience, as in a postsession evaluation. Level 2 requires some sense of change, either a pre-post test (measuring how

effective a leader is prior to and subsequent to coaching) or a change-oriented evaluation. Level 3 is about new behaviors, so it must involve some observation at the workplace over time. Finally, Level 4 requires a determination of the value of the new behaviors, based on the organization's strategic objectives.

Any HRD program should be measured at one or more of these levels. A useful guideline is as follows: the more important and/or general the program, the more levels of measurement should be performed.

What about ROI?

There has been a growing interest in the last decade to create a fifth level to Kirkpatrick's framework, that of return on investment (ROI) for HRD initiatives. The objective is to compute a dollar value of the Level 4 changes, which can be divided by the investment made in the program, to in theory yield ROI. There are many complications in actually doing this.

In theory, here is how one might make such a calculation. Consider a single coach and a single coachee, for a set period of time. Set up the ratio economic gain minus cost divided by cost. The cost may be estimated — in a relatively straightforward manner — from the coach's and coachee's time, the cost of replacing them during coaching activities, and any external consulting cost. The estimate of return is more complicated. This first requires a careful construction of the objectives of the coaching program. These objectives would then create a list of the possible sources of gain for the coaching program. Such a list might include the following:

- Improved retention of the coachee (and of the coach as well!)
- Improved retention of the coachee's reports
- Better management by the coachee
- Improved teamwork at various levels (the coachee's peers, the coachee's reports, and even the reports of the reports)
- Improved performance of these teams as measured by quality, efficiency, innovation, etc.

As you can see, this gets complex very quickly. There is the question of what level to measure: The process? The results? Then there is the question of when to measure; different gains take different amounts of time to become manifest. There is also the issue of interaction; these gains are interrelated, so one can't just total the individual gains. Finally, there is the issue of attribution, perhaps the trickiest of all. Is it that during the time of the coaching, a number of other things occurred — perhaps a layoff, market change, quality program, or change in leadership? Some of these events may move the organization ahead, while others may move things backward or even sideways. How do you break out the effects due to the coaching from the effects of all these other potential performance drivers? The only way that you can be sure of attribution is by using a scientifically controlled experiment, which entails random selection, control groups, and even a double-blind design. In most organizations, such an experiment is not within the realm of possibility.

Despite the difficulties, we suggest that executives include consideration of ROI in their planning of the coaching program. Even with the complexities, going through the thinking will in itself cause the executive sponsors to clarify the objectives of the program, and how they will know whether it is successful.

Using These Principles and Frameworks to Measure the Effectiveness of Coaching

Measurement of coaching value would be indicated at two points:

At a case-by-case point, coach to coachee — In this individual-to-individual situation, you should examine the effects of the coaching experience on each of the individuals, and the Kirkpatrick Levels would be most useful.

At full organizational deployment — Here, you would again use Kirkpatrick, but the ROI would begin to be relevant.

The following are suggestions of how each of these situations might be measured.

Case-by-Case Coaching Effectiveness

In the individual situation, a particular set of objectives for the leader (coachee) have been established. Because coaching is extended over time, there is time to develop and practice new behaviors. Therefore, a postcoaching evaluation could (and should) incorporate reaction, learning, and behavioral change. The fourth Kirkpatrick level — value to the company — would be assessed by determining the degree of accomplishment of the coaching objectives.

It would be important to collect both summative (overall value) and formative (diagnostic) data, so not only could the worth of the program be demonstrated, but also the effectiveness of the program could be illuminated as well.

One useful way to conduct a postcoaching evaluation is for both coach and coachee to complete a self-evaluation instrument, such as that shown in Figure 10.2. (We show one for the coach and a similar one for the leader.) Comparing the views of the coach and the leader on similar items can be very illuminating and can provide valuable diagnostic guidance.

Full Organizational Deployment

In real organizations, resource constraints (dollars, time, etc.) drive any development program, especially programs such as coaching, whose benefits may be manifest only after a period of time. In measurement for coaching, it is crucial to get a large "bang for the buck," to get a large portion of crucial information for a reasonable cost. The measurement as well as the coaching must be efficient. Accordingly, you should extensively use available resources such as data, data collection systems (such as employee surveys), and electronic tools (such as intranets and Web sites).

Measurement should be planned early on, as part of the rollout planning. Obtaining senior management involvement and buy-in is the crucial first step. With the support of the Human Resources leader, senior management needs to answer the following questions at the beginning of the program:

- In which ways is the coaching program intended to benefit the company? How would improvement on the targeted competencies affect financial, operational, customer, and employee indicators?
- What information would tell us if the coaching program is successful at meeting those objectives? How can currently available information be leveraged to provide information on coaching results?
- How can this information be obtained? This step is essentially creating a processing path, that is, a detailed protocol for the

Coach's Self-Evaluation at Each Phase of the Coaching Process
1. Contracting
    - Did you help the leader establish meaningful, manageable goals?
    - Were you clear on what the leader could expect from you as a coach?
    - How effective were you in setting realistic and positive expectations of success?
    - Did you develop a relationship of openness and trust?
2. Data Gathering
    - Did you get clear feedback on competency strengths and development needs for this leader?
    - Did you use the survey feedback to redefine the initial coaching contract?
    - Did you use your own observations as part of your analysis and feedback?
3. Action Planning
    - Did you help the leader identify specific next steps?
    - Did you discuss whether the competencies identified for development are supported by the corporate culture?
    - Did you prepare the leader on how to recover from setbacks?
4. Provide Ongoing Feedback and Opportunity to Reflect
    - Did you assist the leader to reflect on his own blind spots?
    - Were you able to see how the leader's patterns of interactions with others got created in the coaching sessions?
    - Were you able to use those patterns as useful feedback to change the leader's ineffective habits?
5. Create an Ongoing Relationship of Support
    - Did you agree with the leader you are coaching on how your relationship will evolve over time?
    - Did you build in follow-up support?

Leader's Self-Evaluation at Each Phase of the Coaching Process
1. Contracting
    - Did the coach help establish meaningful, manageable goals?
    - Was it clear what you could expect from your coach?
    - How effectively were realistic and positive expectations of success set?
    - Did you develop a relationship of openness and trust with the coach?
2. Data Gathering
    - Did you get clear feedback on your competency strengths and development needs?
    - Was the survey feedback used to redefine the initial coaching contract?
    - Did the coach use her own observations as part of the analysis and feedback?

-- *continued*

Figure 10.2   Coach and leader postevaluation instruments.

3. Action Planning
   - Did the coach help you to identify specific next steps?
   - Did you discuss whether the competencies identified for development are supported by the corporate culture?
   - Did the coach prepare you on how to recover from setbacks?
4. Provide Ongoing Feedback and Opportunity to Reflect
   - Did the coach help you to identify and reflect on patterns of behavior of which you previously were unaware?
   - Did awareness of these patterns serve as useful feedback for you to develop more effective interactions?
5. Create an Ongoing Relationship of Support
   - Did you and the coach discuss and resolve how your relationship would evolve over time?
   - Did the coach build in follow-up support? Is it the right kind of support?

Figure 10.2 (continued)   Coach and leader postevaluation instruments.

design, collection, analysis, reporting, and follow-up of the measurement information.

- How often should this information be communicated, and in what formats and to whom?
- How will this information affect decisions about the ongoing nature of the coaching program?
- Which of Kirkpatrick's levels should be used in measuring the effects of the leadership development? How will each level be implemented?
- Can any part of the program's ROI be calculated?

Ideally, the executives would designate an ongoing steering committee for the coaching initiative. This committee would monitor the initiative, exercise the measurement system, and report to the executives at preplanned intervals. Both the coaching program and the measurement of the coaching program should be evaluated on an ongoing basis.

Reference

1. Ornstein, R., *The Psychology of Consciousness,* Viking Press, New York, 1972.

Chapter 11

Summary: Some Final Thoughts ...

What does being a coach really mean? It is your commitment to others, to give of yourself in the truest sense, so that others will prosper, grow as people, and be able to make a contribution to their businesses and their community. As a coach, you are putting thoughts into action by not only voicing your confidence but also by investing your own time (often our most valued asset) and energy in someone else's success.

This book has focused on one type of coaching, a competency-based approach. I believe that in any organization, this will give you the surest footing to enable you to assist a leader, engage his curiosity, calibrate his emotional response to his business environment, and expand his potential to influence others. In fact, as I discussed, competencies are better predictors of success on the job than intelligence or current fads in leadership style.

The good news is that competencies can be learned, and that as a coach you can guide the leader in a development path that will reap the greatest rewards at work. I am a strong advocate of using a researched competency model as the foundation for coaching because it provides you with a road map for leadership success in your unique organization.

The core to coaching for competencies is getting feedback from others. Feedback is critical, both for performance improvement and for making good decisions about our careers. The essence of feedback is to see ourselves the way others see us, and to use data along with insight into what we like to do (often reflected in our motives) and what we want to do (often reflected in our values). Coaching for competencies means effectively guiding your leaders through this feedback process, helping them formulate action plans, and then observing the leaders putting these development ideas into action. Without coaching, the feedback leaders tend to get is directed more to tangible results than to the seemingly more elusive personal behaviors that garnered those results. Coaching for competencies provides both the tools and the language to talk about important elements of emotional intelligence that are often instrumental to a leader's growth.

The hallmark of adult development is whether someone is able to look at himself honestly and redirect his efforts where needed. By coaching, you have the opportunity to assist in unlocking this potential. You can inspire others to believe that they don't have to settle for second-rate success or uncomfortable situations at work. Coaching leaders helps them look at the difference they can make for the people they manage, the organizations they lead, the customers who depend on their services, the investors who support their business, and the communities of which they are a part.

For Coaches Old and New — Key Points to Remember

For those of you that have been coaching for a long time, I hope you have found this book refreshing and reinforcing for the work that you do, with a few new ideas or tips to add to your tool kit. For those of you who are new to coaching, I have laid out a road map that you can use on a day-to-day basis. Remember, a part of coaching can be an impromptu chat, making use of the "coachable moments" as well as a planned series of meetings that are scheduled to track progress over time. A couple of key points bear repeating:

- **Coaching is not one-stop shopping** — While I believe that coachable moments are critical because they are in the context of the immediacy of the situation, a single discussion is unlikely to have a significant impact. Coachable moments should be a part of a larger coaching strategy in which the coach and the leader partner to formulate and work on specific competency development goals. The following five steps comprise a process that requires an investment of time to realize results in sustained behavioral change: (1) contracting, (2) data gathering, (3) action planning, (4) providing ongoing feedback and an opportunity to reflect, and (5) creating an ongoing relationship of support.

■ **Take the time to build the relationship** — People do not want advice or criticism from someone they don't like or trust. Connect to the person, not only with your ideas but with your heart. Each person shows how he or she cares differently. Bring your unique personality to the coaching relationship, your "authentic presence." At the same time, honor the uniqueness of the person you are coaching and appreciate that she may have a different perspective on a situation based on a different set of life experiences and values.

■ **Coaching is more asking than telling** — Developing empathy involves excellent listening skills that are the hallmark of a good coach. One of the things I had to learn early in my career was to resist the temptation to try to immediately fix someone's problem when he or she came to me to vent frustrations. Often when you simply ask probing questions, the person you are coaching can begin to get a broader perspective on a situation and enlarge his scope of options to solve a difficult problem. As a coach, if you jump in too quickly, you can shut down that analysis process prematurely.

■ **Coaching is not the solution for everything** — There are times for every coach when a leader may remain defensive and not be prepared to do anything differently despite your best efforts or feedback that you provide. To some extent, the old cliché "you can lead a horse to water, but you can't force him to drink" applies to coaching. We are all ultimately accountable for our own behavior and our own choices. If a leader is receptive to your coaching, it is certainly a more gratifying experience. However, if the leader doesn't make the changes in the time frame you have laid out, it does not mean that you failed to make an impact. If you have done your job, your impact may be felt long after the coaching relationship has ceased. Some problems, even at the leadership level, are just a symptom of larger issues that an individual is experiencing in her life. If you are a line manager and issues come up that may require medical or other types of professional attention, don't hesitate to seek additional help.

As a Coach, What's in It for You?

In the workplace, coaching can be one of the most gratifying relationships you can have. I believe that you can learn from every person that you meet, although it may not be completely obvious at first. Years ago when I was still in my early 20s, I briefly taught English at Olney High School, where I met a young man named Darryl, who was from the Caribbean. Darryl was floundering in the class I taught, and I spent time getting to know him and trying to inspire in him the motivation to reach higher in his classroom performance and in life. In the process, Darryl shared with me stories about a lovely spot on his island that was still undeveloped and not well known by tourists. Being young and adventurous, I took a vacation later that year to that same spot. In addition to having a wonderful vacation, my belief in looking to everyone I meet as a source of ideas, wisdom, or even fun "tips" got reinforced for a lifetime. I don't see learning as a one-way street. Granted, as an executive coach, I am there to assist others with how they can be more effective at work or to find a next career step that will be more satisfying. But in the richness of getting to know other people and understanding how their experiences have shaped who they are and how they see the world, I expand who I am.

In the short term, coaching can simply help you get the job done. Coaching can result in more effective leaders who will promote better morale and a higher level of commitment among the entire workforce. When people are more committed, they tend to be more productive and produce better results. In the longer term, coaching is also a process where you have the opportunity to give back and to pass on the knowledge and insight that others have given you. By contributing to others becoming stronger leaders, you are building a living legacy for your business and industry.

I am as excited today as I have ever been about the opportunity we all have to continue to change and evolve as we grow older, and in the process I have become excited rather than discouraged by life's challenges. Coaching and teaching others to be better coaches are outlets for that passion.

Index

A

Academics, coaching success and, 9
Accountability, 183
Achievement
    coaching strategies for, 75–76
    description of, 75
    Generation X, 181
    motivation through, 145–146
Action planning, 50–54
Affiliation, 146, 181
Altruism, 167
Authentic, 27–28

B

Baby Boomers
    characteristics of, 176, 178–179
    coaching of, 177, 179–181
    definition of, 176
Behavioral event interview, 29–30
Behaviorally researched competency
        models
    advantages and disadvantages of, 92,
        99–101
    creation of, 97–98
    description of, 97
    implementation of, 98–99
    principles of, 98
Best practices competency models
    advantages and disadvantages of, 92–94
    description of, 92
    tailoring of, 94–97

Blaming, 37
Business problem, competencies reframed
        as, 22–24, 32–34

C

Career development
    assignments for, 166–167
    coaching benefits for, 168–169, 173–174
    competencies, 160–162
    expanding choices for, 171–173
    high-potential leader, 164–167
    mid-career leader, 167–168
    motivation, 158–160
    opportunities, 162–164
    outside coach used for, 169–171, 174
    overview of, 153–154
    pitfalls associated with, 173
    summary of, 173–174
    values, 155–157
Change
    adaptation to, 136–139
    evaluation of, 199
    motivation for, 51
Cluster of competencies, *See* Competency
        clusters
Coach
    advice giving by, 14
    as leader, 3–4
    external executive, 7, 15–16
    internal staff as, 15
    leader and, relationship between, 45–46
    mentor vs., 165